WATER WALKER

WATER WALKER

CATHERINE BLANCH

MURRE PUBLISHING

Copyright © 2024 by Catherine Blanch

All biblical quotations are taken from the HOLY BIBLE, New International Version, Copyright © 1973, 1978, 1984, 2011, International Bible Society. Used by permission. All rights reserved.

All rights reserved.

No part of this book may be reproduced in any form or by any electronic or mechanical means, including information storage and retrieval systems, without written permission from the author, except for the use of brief quotations in articles and/or reviews.

MURRE PUBLISHING

ISBN 9798328678155

*For all the water walkers-
in a storm, upon the waves,
and exploring new shores with Jesus.*

CONTENTS

Introduction	9
1. Seed of Desire	13
2. Born Again Baby	21
3. Hearing His Voice	29
4. A Watery Grave	35
5. New Beginnings	39
6. Longing to Meet	45
7. Cheese for That Whine	47
8. Baptized in Fire	53
9. Good Father	57
10. Julia	61
11. The Gift of Brokenness	65
12. The Return of Julia	71
13. Heart Redemption	75
14. Under His Wing	83
15. Two Things in My Hands	87
16. Called Where No Path is Laid	91
17. Into the Deep	97
18. Be Holy as I Am Holy	107
19. This is War	115
20. Storms and Authority	125
21. School of the Holy Spirit	131
22. Parade of Demons	135
23. Knots in a Net	137
24. Good News for All	139
25. People are Flailing, Help Them	143
26. The In-Between Space	147
27. Burn the Plough, Offer the Oxen	149
28. Doing What You Say, Even When It's Weird	151
29. One Dream for Another	153
30. Israel—The Heart of God	161
31. Angel on the Bus	165

32. Ancient Paths	167
33. Snow Prayer	171
34. Vision of a Mountain	175
35. An Open Door	177
36. Worship Breaker	183
37. The Underground Church	187
38. Portals of Heaven	189
39. Desert Prayer	193
40. The Kingdom is Here	197
41. Murre	201
42. Jesus in the Prayer Room	203
43. Upon the Waves	207
44. When He Speaks, the Sea Obeys	211
45. Killing the Snake	217
46. My Grace is Sufficient	219
47. The Nations are Calling	223
48. The Groom is Coming	229
Afterword	235

INTRODUCTION

What does it look like to live with radical faith in God? Are the stories in the Bible dusty legends from years ago to reflect upon in a post-miracle world where God is no longer engaging with creation? Or is God still active today?

The other day, I talked with a friend who lamented that many churches focus only on how God moved thousands of years ago. We marvel at the Biblical miracles and multiplications from ages ago. We savor the stories of demons fleeing, seas parting, and angels appearing. Giants fall. Donkeys talk. It's like visiting a museum and looking at paintings guarded by a velvet rope. But where is the gallery for today's modern miracles?

Where are the oceans waiting to be walked upon? Do we believe God is still moving today, searching for people willing to step out in radical faith? The church needs to know its authority in Jesus. She needs to know the tools and tactics from God for victory in the battle.

What does it look like to walk upon the deep with Jesus? How do we walk in unencumbered faith? Do we rest on the laurels of unmerited salvation, reclining in our comfortable homes and observing the demise at our doorsteps with half-interested apathy? The shroud of complacency must be discarded to fulfill destinies as God's children. God poured His Spirit into us so that we could shift Kingdoms.

Jesus accomplished everything through His resurrection. He gave us the blueprint and authority. When we are born again, our former lives are crucified in Christ—we become filled with Jesus; we live in Him.

Jesus told us we could do even greater things in His name. It is not for passivity we are reborn. We emerge as infants from the womb of salvation but are to become mature sons of God who represent their Father in Heaven well. We reign with Jesus *now* and not merely in the world to come. We dismantle the forces of Hell. We set captives free, leading them through the gate of Jesus into supernatural living. The church is a threat to the powers of evil, so much so that Hell tries to keep God's army from realizing its power, and few churches preach the whole story. Living a life of faith is not warming pews but breaking chains. Extravagant faith looks like walking on water so giants would fall.

Freedom wins. Victory is guaranteed. Faith is required. There is plundering, rescuing, and warring. There is extravagant, generous love. Hell does not win. Jesus already has the victory.

Men and women who walk in extravagant faith become water walkers with Jesus. We think about the Billy Grahams and Mother Theresas, wishing there were more like them. Yet, *everyone* is invited to share in this reward, leaning on God as mountains fling themselves into the sea. These water walkers move across the globe at God's prompting. They sell their homes to pioneer new global frontiers so God's Kingdom can advance. They start home churches in their local communities and reach out to their neighbors with the love of God. They live as passionate bond-servants to King Jesus with a sensitive spirit to hear His voice. And they can't do this without an intimate walk with God. Like Adam and Eve, who walked in the garden with God, we sense God's presence. We respond to His voice. And we delight in Him.

Every one of us is invited to walk on water with Jesus.

In the Bible, Jesus challenged a wealthy young man to sell his possessions, give everything to the poor, and follow Jesus. When the man turned away sadly, Jesus' disciples wondered how anyone could fulfill such a demanding sacrifice. *Yet we are not our own.* On the other side of surrender is an abundant and fruitful life of faith waiting to be grasped. The sacrifice is worth it.

This book is my testimony of putting one foot in front of the other, taking baby steps with my hand outstretched to God as a toddler learning to walk. I was content in the world until one day when I wasn't. I became like that rich young man who wanted the "more" that Jesus offered. I was provoked until I gave in because the deep waters looked much more exciting than the mundane world, and I wanted to experience everything Jesus offered. I wanted an overflowing glass and not just a glass half-full.

Jesus reaches His hand to you. Will you step out of the boat? There's no telling what God has waiting for you. A fantastic adventure awaits. Those first baby steps are the hardest, but your faith will soar when you see the waves below you. Picture yourself on a fishing boat at sea. You lift your foot over the boat's edge to take that first scary step. The waves lap your toes as your foot comes down upon the water. Jesus watches you intently, with a smile in His eyes and a parent's joy at a baby's first steps. He coaxes you gently as your eyes are fixed on Him.

Jesus says, "You can do it. Take My hand."

1

SEED OF DESIRE

Have you ever wondered about the faith of a child? When you were young, you were fed by a spoon and nourished so you could grow. You depended on others and were sustained by their provision. As you grew in body, you also grew in Spirit, and your independence from others diminished while your desire to know your place in the world increased. God planted a seed of desire inside you for you to know Him. This desire has always been inside you. It's there because God made you and breathed life into you. There are reports of infants smiling and talking with invisible spirits from their cribs. Some Jewish sages teach that when a baby is born, an angel taps it on the head so it forgets the knowledge of Heaven to relearn God's mysteries and majesty through its life on Earth. The search for truth and wisdom from God is in the seed, the DNA from Heaven, that each of us contains. The seed will grow depending on the foundation planted and the sustenance given. A seed can grow on rocky soil and healthy dirt with enough light, water, and care.

Every person's faith journey with God is that seed sprouted and allowed to grow. Seeds are discussed often in the Bible.

Isaiah 28 talks about planting and farming, explaining how a farmer plants different seeds in their way so they will grow. Caraway is sown, and cummin is scattered. Wheat and barley have plots, and spelt is sown in their fields. God instructs the farmer and teaches him the right way. Caraway seeds are not threshed; they are beaten out with a rod. Cummin is not rolled by a cartwheel but beaten with a stick.

These are from the wisdom of God, who counsels the farmer to cultivate each unique seed. So, regardless of your spiritual nourishment when young, God plans to develop the seed that He planted within you uniquely.

Jesus spoke about how the growth of seeds was affected by the foundation sown. He addressed the worries of the world that could snuff out the vibrant life of the seed and how a tiny seed could grow into a large tree when given attention and care to grow. He spoke of faith as a little seed that could uproot large mountains.

That which is the seed within us contains the potential for extravagant faith in God. This is God's marvelous design when we cultivate that waiting to be birthed within us. Jesus told His disciples in Matthew 17:20:

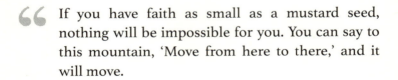
> If you have faith as small as a mustard seed, nothing will be impossible for you. You can say to this mountain, 'Move from here to there,' and it will move.

Jesus taught about extravagant faith. Heaven was within His listeners' reach if they would hear and respond. A delicate, papery sheath was the thin barrier from which a small seed would burst forth to penetrate the soil and bear roots and limbs.

An unencumbered freckle of faith would bring to life an enormous tree.

Seed of Desire

Children have a beautiful way of realizing that faith. In the Bible, people brought little children to be blessed by Jesus. Jesus scolded the disciples when they tried to interfere.

> Let the little children come to me, for the Kingdom of God belongs to children.
> (Mark 10:13-16)

I had a dream once where God showed me how each person is like a child before God and how we can see them through His eyes. In the dream, I was walking down an alley, looking for the entrance to a church. I stepped over trash cans strewn and walked by mechanics disassembling a car engine. Two burly thugs of men jumped out in front of me, blocking me. I tried to scream but could only whisper. The mechanics nearby watched but continued working on the car. The men grabbed my shoulders and were about to hurt me.

> *My voice squeaked out, "Get behind me, Satan. The blood of Jesus covers me." At this, their hands fell limp to their sides, their mouths agape in confusion. I continued, now boldly, "Do you want to be free? Jesus can set you free."*

At that moment, they began sobbing. While they did, their bodies aged backward, and they became two wide-eyed toddlers. This is how God saw them before the scars of life wounded them and robbed them of God's seed of promise. I had compassion and scooped them both under my arms to walk toward that mysterious church.

Down the alley was an unmarked warehouse door, open enough to see hundreds of people buzzing. An enormous buffet was there, and the tables were piled high with food. People circled inside, walking and talking with overflowing plates. I nudged the door open, and a light beam from the alley caught their attention. When the crowd saw the two toddlers with me, they seemed to recognize them as familiar faces of fear. I slowly approached the buffet and piled food for the boys and me.

I sat in a dark corner, away from a hundred staring eyes. After a while, as we nibbled in the shadows, the room shifted from coifed professional adults to bumbling toddlers. Everyone laughed and spilled food as they tried to walk and hold plates. No one was afraid, and perceptions vanished. Weathered faces became young.

The potential of promise is within us—redemption's hope is in every breath. God redeems the dark alleys and battle-scarred minds. He pours healing light so seeds can grow. He wants His children to know Him.

Letting God's light into places with locked doors takes courage. Hearts can be healed when God's light is invited in. Every seed starts small, but before you know it, you will speak to mountains and soar in the Spirit with Jesus.

CAN you imagine what it was like to be among the crowds in the Bible who witnessed Jesus performing miracles? Imagine if you were there and saw Jesus multiply a few fish and loaves and feed thousands of hungry travelers. How do you think you would respond if you were there? Would you follow Him from town to town, uprooting your family and work? Would you be filled with faith, or would you walk away sad? Every encounter is a choice to trust and follow God or doubt and disbelieve. Our reaction to God's reality doesn't change His reality; it just suspends our belief. God is merciful, thankfully, and meets with each of us at the level we can receive. He doesn't drown a seedling with too much water at once.

Seed of Desire

Children are good at cultivating seeds. They don't generally have the baggage adults might have. When I was nine, Jesus healed me with a tenderness that allowed my faith in God to germinate. I was on a family trip to Virginia to visit relatives. One night at dinner, I hurt my finger, cutting it deeply with a knife. It was a severe cut, and I was crying as my aunt and uncle raced me upstairs to clean my wound. After bandaging me up, they prayed for me, holding my hand.

They asked God to heal my finger. They called on the name of Jesus, and power surged through my body as they did. I stared at them both, wide-eyed. I struggled to sleep all night because I couldn't wait until morning to check my finger.

The moment my eyes opened, I unwrapped the gauze from my finger. There was no cut. There was no blood. I examined all my fingers, confused and excited. I ran downstairs and told everyone.

THE FOLLOWING YEAR, we visited my grandparents' house in Queens, New York, with my family and my relatives from Virginia. There were many people and not enough rooms, so I was told I had to sleep in the basement. No one liked sleeping down there, especially if you were the only one there. As cars drove on the road, the headlights created ominous shadows that bounced off the walls and cast long dark beams over eerie velvet paintings and stark tiles. Too many shadows and shapes play on a child's imagination. I couldn't close my eyes.

I ran upstairs crying. My uncle gently led me back to the basement, although I was dragging my legs. That was not the answer I'd hoped for. He tucked me in and promised I'd be safe. My young eyes shot him a panicked look of doubt. What he said next, I'll never forget.

> *"Jesus is always with you. When you can't feel His presence, close your hand into a ball like this and make a fist. Say Jesus, and you will know He is with you when your hand gets warm."*

I tried it. It worked. Left alone to sleep, I made a fist several times and said, *Jesus*. My hand warmed, and I was able to sleep. It was childlike faith, and the fears were lifting away.

I WAS TAUGHT about Jesus as a child. I loved God with my young heart, but life choices would steer me off that path in my teens and early adulthood before I recognized my desperate need for God. I made terrible choices and became surrounded by darkness like the thugs in the dream. Fear, torment, and anxiety are real entities. Jesus dealt with evil spirits more than anything else He did, and He commanded them to leave. The healing can happen when the house is clean. In His mercy, God hovers over His children to lead them to His love for them and protect them from the evil that tries to snuff out life and light.

I am so thankful God never gave up on me. When David declares in the Bible he'd prefer to be a doorkeeper in God's house, he was saying on the spectrum of God's perfect light and evil's darkness, even being in the doorway of light was better than its absence. And better was one day there than a thousand anywhere else.

The innocent faith I had as a little girl was stuffed under layers of independence and tangled roots of defiance from years of running the wrong way. My teenage years were awkward and shy, and there was constant tension growing up. My self-worth teetered on a rocky seesaw. I was a punk and got into heavy rock music. I saw a therapist. I bucked against authority. I partied. I messed around with the new age and was understimulated at school, even in the advanced classes. During college, I studied for a semester in Spain, catching a glimpse of freedom. After university, I packed my possessions and drove from New York to Seattle to make something of myself.

∽

I WAS WOUNDED, running away, and didn't know where I was going.

2

BORN AGAIN BABY

My story started to shift toward God. I was in my late twenties, living in Seattle. I was looking for a purpose in life, working hard but partying harder. My heart was yet to be surrendered to God, but I searched for and even tried out a few churches occasionally. But my bad choices still outweighed my heart, and it was as if I was floating downstream with all the other dead fish instead of swimming against the current. The world's mire extended to me a buffet with little flavor to perpetuate a cycle of sin and self-loathing.

It was autumn in Washington State, with beautiful foliage and evergreens, and I was going on a camping weekend with a group of friends in the Cascade Mountains. My friend Mike and I were in charge of bringing sodas, but we didn't stop at a store in Seattle to avoid the rush-hour traffic. The further we drove from the city, the sparser the landscape became. We were in a remote wilderness, miles from signs of civilization, and our mission to bring drinks seemed hopeless.

I noticed an off-season ski lodge at the mountain's edge seemingly abandoned. I told Mike to park and wait so I could check if they sold soda. The door was unlocked, but no one was inside. I called out. No one answered. I went upstairs into a large open dining room. I walked to the large back windows. There was a line of toboggans stacked against the wall facing empty slopes. Lost in thought, I started pushing buttons on juice machines in the cafeteria to see if they dispensed anything.

Suddenly, the room shifted, and voices filled the room. The floorboards rumbled like waves under my feet. I couldn't stand up. A voice from the invisible space screamed at me to get out of the building, and I ran down the plank stairs with my knees knocking, racing for the door. Something evil was breathing over my shoulder; I dared not look.

I jumped in the van and told Mike to drive fast. He told me there was no earthquake, and the ground did not shake outside. He told me no trucks hit the building, and no cars full of people showed up while I was inside. What I experienced was the horror of demonic spirits that didn't like my being there. I wanted to know more about the spirit world that, until then, was just a figment of Hollywood.

As I read the Bible, I was surprised at how many times Jesus encountered and dealt with evil and unclean spirits. Doors I had opened foolishly to the occult over the years became very real, very fast, and I was starting to realize that the invisible spirit world can often be more tangible than the material world we live in. God allowed the experience in the abandoned ski lodge so I would see my desperation for God and someday let His light shine into my heart.

I started to want to know Him.

I was nearing the time in my life when I would finally surrender my heart to the Lord so the healing could begin. Someone told me no matter where you go, there you are, which didn't make me feel better. Deep down, I knew I was trying to run away from myself. But I wouldn't be able to stuff things forever, and God was patiently waiting for me to get to the bottom of the belly of a whale so He could spit me on dry land. That whale was a busy Seattle bar on a Saint Patrick's night with carousing friends drinking pints of beer.

It was a fateful night, at the time horrible, but looking back, destined for my rebirth in God, so in the grand scheme of things, a red-letter day. I was in a busy bar celebrating with friends, wall-to-wall with people. I pushed my way to the front of the bar so I could yell my order over all the noise when a drunk guy pushed me. I pushed him back. It turned into a push-match, and the next thing I knew, a bouncer kicked both of us out onto the empty street despite my protests that I wasn't at fault.

My friends waved me a nonchalant goodbye from the large corner table. They didn't want to give up to leave with me. I walked home alone and angry, feeling rejected by my friends and wronged in many ways. I brewed and stewed in the biggest pity party, sulking for several days and crying.

I wasn't made of as thick of skin as I pretended to have. Inside was a fragile girl who'd taken many beatings in life and whose heart felt like a piece of cube steak beaten flat and barely ticking. My spirit felt limp and lifeless. I cried out to the mysterious God that I wasn't sure heard me. A film of all the sins I'd ever done played before me like a movie in my mind. I was broken and unraveled to my core.

Like Jonah in the Bible, I was at the bottom of my ocean in a belly full of slime. I realized it was time to get launched on land.

The following week, cheeks stained from days of crying, I walked my chocolate lab before work. On the roadside was a dead cat, and I immediately recognized that it belonged to my twenty-something neighbor, Katie. With a lump in my throat, I knocked on her door to tell her the news of her cat. I went to work with a heavy heart, thinking about her and how awful that was. It was the first time in a long time that I had thought about somebody besides myself. Later that day, I gave her a little candle and a card to brighten her day.

The smallest gesture of seemingly insignificant kindness can unravel the mess of tangle and create a ripple on the water that sets you on a recourse of life. Like the whale and the shore, one moment can change everything forever.

Katie's reply to me was that moment—my rock bottom launched me into a new and brighter future. All she did was put a notecard in my mailbox, thanking me for letting God's light shine through me and including a Bible verse.

I drank deep into the breath of hopeful life that I read on that card. I felt like Jonah sucking air and ready to stop running. I wanted to ask Katie everything, especially why a young, stylish, seemingly normal girl like her would write me Bible verses in a card. That was not normal in my world. Katie and I started talking daily, and she did her best to answer my questions.

I started going to a church again and realized the Bible was full of broken people and not perfect saints like I'd been taught. They overcame challenging circumstances and made mistakes; their pursuit of God and humility to serve and follow Him became the bedrock of Biblical faith. I would learn that the gaping hole in my heart could only be filled by Jesus. Only He could bring peace and stillness to the waves in my deepest ocean.

The first chapter of Colossians describes Jesus as a hero who rescues His beloved from a fiery hell-breathing dragon. This is the story of the rescue of Christ's corporate bride, which every Christian comprises. Jesus' obedience to death on the cross represents that glorious rescue mission.

We are like that bride trapped in a furnace that Jesus reaches out to save. The power of hell is subject to Jesus because He was victorious at Calvary. No power can stand up to Him—He alone is the King of kings. When we try to live separate from God, we have no protection from the power of Hell. Only with God are we restored to the design intended for us when life first entered our lungs.

Like an injured baby bird in God's hand, your racing heartbeat from a mangled ribcage starts to steady, bones heal, and stressed-out limbs unclench in His palm.

We get to the end of ourselves. We find out God is all we need. God's peace surpasses understanding. You can draw deep breaths and taste freedom.

OVER THE FOLLOWING MONTHS, as a baby Christian, I learned to walk and depend on the mercy and patience of God. The enemy raged against me, and thirty nights of demonic nightmares left me miserable, almost giving up on God. Night after night, I awoke in a panic and sweat. The nightmares were terrifying, and I hated going to sleep. Demons who had legal permission to torment me were putting up a fight to scare me from pursuing my fledgling faith. They didn't want to go. When I awoke from the fears, my hands grabbed for my shiny new Bible on the bedside table; I would pray for hours until the darkness passed. I didn't know how to pray, but I instinctively knew I had to grab the Bible and read it aloud.

It was a battle for my soul. I felt it intensely. Evil powers do not willingly relinquish their prey. And I had unknowingly opened many demonic doorways through naively foolish sins such as Ouija boards and new-age teachings. I had picked up channeling books and foolishly read the 'prayers' to invite spirit guides *that were not from God*. I had exercised powers from the occult and had played with fire—now the enemy was bent on burning me. As the demonic nightmares persisted, I knew intuitively they would stop *only* if I stopped pursuing God. I could hear whispers during the nightmares when I pleaded for it to stop, stop, stop, as they taunted me to forget about God.

Two words change the trajectory of a life: *But God!* Such a wonderful sentence that changes circumstances from drastic to hopeful. God can do anything in His infinite mercy and love. No matter how far you run in the other direction, no distance is too far for God to reach and save you.

But God!

The truth is, those evil spirits were always there tormenting me, making me depressed and lonely and missing out on so much of the life God wanted to bless me with. But the evil spirits had not been poked with a stick until then, and leaving their home (in me) was not a threat until God's glorious light started pouring into me. Even though I got close to giving up on God from the oppressing nightmares for thirty nights straight, I made it through to the other side with God's grace. The light exposed the dark that had to go. What a beautiful image.

I remember staying in a fourteenth-century pension on the island of Crete. I didn't realize the place was full of roaches until I walked to the bathroom in the dark without putting on my glasses. It wasn't until we checked out that my friend told me how gross the place was. She saw the bugs because she put the lights on at night while I slept. They were there the whole time: the light exposed everything.

One night, the nightmares stopped. I slept soundly, and the battle for my soul was won. God taught me like a newborn baby that I had to learn to run to Him for nourishment. The Word of God would become my safe place. Thinking back on it now, I imagine with humility that the angels God appointed to me likely had a beating on my behalf all those nights. I'm sure they were relieved when the shadows were defeated, and I surrendered fully to the light of God.

When we invite Jesus to be our Savior, we learn to bow our knees to Him as King. It's not just lip service; there's a reaction.

If our lives are not changed, who is lord of our lives? Who we once were is crucified with Christ—dead and buried—so that the new man rising in us is filled with His power, presence, and peace. We become like babies again, learning to breathe, eat, and walk again. The old nature is destroyed and will never rise again. Jesus teaches us how to battle and win, taking captive thoughts and desires so that only Jesus is on the throne of our hearts. The old corpse cannot rise; that fallen flesh is dead and buried in a watery grave. This is a truth Satan does not want us to grasp; he wants to keep people trapped, thinking they're barely alive and that he could grab them back at any moment. But our salvation through a heart surrendered to Jesus is fixed and secure.

Our lives will grow to reflect the fruit of our faith, but as long as we keep our eyes on Jesus, we do not sink; this is the blessed assurance of which we sing. This is the hope we profess without wavering. Only one name carries authority over every realm on Heaven and Earth and under the earth: the name of Jesus.

THE MORE JESUS HEALED ME, the more I offered Him my heart. It was like when Jesus offered to wash Peter's feet.

Peter said, "No way."

Then Jesus said, "Well unless I wash your feet, you can have no part of Me."

And Peter said, "Well, please wash all of me!"

I saw the progress in one part of me and was so grateful; I wanted Jesus to heal every bit of me. My heart was all I could offer Him, the wellspring of all my hopes, dreams, and even disappointments. It was the only thing I had to give. The more I invited Him to live inside of me, the more exciting the adventure became. For a year or so after getting born again and trying to find my new identity out in Seattle, I even went back to the bars and parties to witness to friends in my newfound enthusiasm for God.

I loved wearing a black T-shirt with a big letter M for Mars Hill to parties. I would walk up to total strangers at parties and say,

 "Do you know what this 'M' stands for? Mars Hill. Can I tell you what happened on Mars Hill? A whole bunch of philosophers who knew every academic had erected shrines to hundreds of their gods. They had this one shrine inscribed to an 'unknown god' just in case they missed one and didn't want to incur its wrath. I am here to tell you about that unknown God, the only God ever!"

I was so filled with zeal for what God did in my life I wanted the world to know. I had many crazy prayer times with people smoking dope and wanting to give it up, things like that. Bringing God's light into dark corners that I once frequented in the darkness was a tremendous joy. I was living proof of God's miracles. I loved sharing my story with the people I used to hang out with. If He could save this mess of what I was, He could undoubtedly save anyone.

Because of all that God had done in my life, I became a threat to the enemy's camp and a zealous evangelist.

Flavors were flavorful, and colors were colorful. The world I thought was a buffet to the palette was evident in its squalor.

I WANTED everyone to experience the radiance of a life filled with God's light and love through Jesus.

3

HEARING HIS VOICE

At that time, I started to feel a nudge that I didn't shake. It was a strong desire to move back to New York. That was weird because I had been enjoying living in Seattle for eight years, and it didn't make sense to pick up and go 'home' again. The urge would not leave, and eventually, I pulled my roots up, packed a U-haul, and headed back to New York to be part of a church plant and be closer to family again.

I drove with Duncan across the Cascades, Dakota Plains, and Rocky Mountains, my heart full of anticipation and adventure. He hung his head out the window in the breeze. We both tasted freedom and hope.

The car broke down a few times with crazy stories like sleeping on a couch at a tow-truck driver's taxidermy ranch as coyotes howled outside or my dad catching a last-minute flight to Rapid City to help me when my transmission died in the Badlands. We towed the dead car two thousand miles to the East Coast.

But nothing could stop me, for I was returning to my home state where the Lord was calling me, and even though my faith was a fledgling little seedling sprouting from the dirt, I felt like I could hurl mountains.

When I got to New York, I got the car fixed and stayed as a guest with a pastor's family for three months while I looked for work. Every day, I looked for housing and work. I got more discouraged every day. Doubt crept to try to drown hope. Did God really tell me to move? Why were things not working out? The dot.com Seattle boom was a vibrant and thriving workforce and music scene for a girl in her twenties. Now, in upstate New York, where things should have been easier and slower, I couldn't get meetings, and there was a reticency for West Coast progression in a nichey handshake community.

Things aren't always easy when we follow God. I complained like a whiny kid. God was teaching me to be unshackled from my unreliable dependence that *I* was the mistress of my destiny. Living a life surrendered to Jesus meant laying down my expectations. The value I'd placed on my professional accolades was hot air from insecurity. God didn't care about how many college degrees I had or that I was a go-getter. He wasn't impressed by awards in the business world from someone trying to make a name for herself. That was a shifting sand foundation. Jesus needed to rebuild my life on Himself if my life was to be overflowing. Self-importance was only insecurity masked—it needed to be thrown back on the potter's wheel and reshaped. In the heat of a kiln, that bubbled-up clay would shatter. At its root was pride and a childish pertinence to think of salvation in Jesus as a box on a list of life goals to tick. That's how it is sometimes in our baby steps with Jesus. Doesn't a baby tumble over and over trying to walk? It's all part of the process, but the goal is to keep growing and learning how to run.

I have a funny image sometimes of a lump of disfigured clay hoisting itself up to the potter's wheel, with every ounce of energy, sighing as it reaches the summit, and with its final fling, beseeching the potter with a lisping voice like Sylvester, the cat.

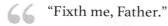 "Fixth me, Father."

It makes me laugh because that's how desperation looks when we see ourselves as that lump of clay needing remolding.

IN THE BOOK OF GENESIS, Jacob wrestled with the Lord, contending with God for his breakthrough. Like Jacob, we must push through every barrier to walk into God's plans. He desires that these dreams manifest; they will when we press past the flailing.

One day, tired from apartment and job searching for weeks without success, I pulled the car to the side of the road and cried out in a flailing prayer to Jesus. After a while, a beautiful peace overtook me. A fresh wave of hope stilled my mind and filled me with renewed trust in God. I wiped my eyes and started the car back on the road again. One mile further down the road, I was compelled by a strong yet invisible force to turn down a small street on the banks of a river. As I drove slowly, I saw the most idyllic road. Pastel brownstones of yellow and blue lined the river with a green expanse of trimmed lawns to the water's edge, and rowboats pulled ashore. I wondered what a pretty street it was and how lucky I might be to live there. Glancing at the houses, I noticed a handwritten 'for rent' sign taped on one door. I called the number, and within an hour, I had signed rental papers for my new home. The price was better than any apartment I had seen, and the apartment was better looking, with twelve-foot high ceilings and enormous windows facing the river.

The sign was only posted on the door that morning, and the

owner said they did not advertise online or in papers. It was the perfect timing; only God could have lined it up for me to drive down that street that day. It was His plan; I just had to let Him navigate. His hand of providence was guiding me, whispering, Trust Me.

~

WHEN WE FOLLOW GOD, He directs our steps if we let Him. He might speak through a person, a billboard, or a Bible verse that makes our hearts thump. When we earnestly seek God's guidance, He is faithful to answer.

I was settling into my new apartment but still had not found a job. I wondered if I hadn't heard God correctly (oh, how quickly we doubt), and I applied for a job in New York City, two hours south. Although I had just signed a lease, I wondered if Albany was a stepping stone to bring me back east. I got a call back for an interview the next week and—confused but wondering—went to sleep.

The brightest light, brighter than the sun, awakened me. My bedroom was glowing. I squinted to see a large white form at the end of my bed. I felt like I was under an enormous X-ray machine, and every thought and secret deed was exposed through that light. I tried to sink my body into the mattress, desperate to hide somehow. If I could have crawled inside or under my bed, I would have. Then I heard words spoken—though I don't know if it was a thought or an audible voice—still, they were spoken with clarity that left no room for doubt.

"Do not go to New York City."

I knew it was either an angel of God or the Lord Himself speaking. After a long time, the light left my room, and all was still and dark again. I couldn't wait until morning to cancel my interview. I didn't even worry about an excuse because the message was given with urgent clarity.

I may not understand why it was so significant that I did not move again then, but I knew God was trying to get my attention and keep me on His path. God knows what He is doing and promises to lead us like a good shepherd. Knowing He can and will redirect us when we need it brings great comfort.

∼

WITHIN A FEW WEEKS, things opened up. I got a full-time contract job while picking up consulting work for public relations. If that wasn't enough, I relaunched my jazz career with a new band. One thing about jazz music is not staying within the safety net of musical rules but waterskiing on the side of the boat to make your own waves in the water. It builds on a foundation of theory that takes musicians to a higher plane of ability, adjusting chords and scatting solos by reinventing melodies in a structure. They don't break the rules, but they play outside the lines. I was learning that God doesn't follow my expectations. He would always be faithful to His nature, but my limited understanding couldn't hold Him back.

∼

I HAD to let Him lead me and teach me.

4

A WATERY GRAVE

Around this time, I decided to get baptized to confess my faith publicly. The Bible made it clear that it was a decision each person had to make on their own when they were old enough to know what it meant to invite Jesus to be their Savior and Lord. I struggled with the idea of standing in front of people, but I knew an unspeakable joy awaited me on the other side of the water.

As I remember that day that I publicly declared Jesus is my Lord, it was as if I could see the shimmer of a corpse fading like a shadow into the waters—the shadow of who I once was, sinking into oblivion. To this day, when the enemy tries to dig up accusations of that old person who was crucified with Christ, I can remind him that Jesus buried that sucker in a watery grave.

On that life-changing day, I emerged from the waters of baptism glowing. I remember wearing black clothing and going into the water; I chose white when I changed into dry clothes. Even though I couldn't explain it, I knew what I did was a moment that would change my eternity. It was as if the air in my lungs tasted different.

Something holy happened in that water.

The powers of Hell had to let me go. I felt an exchange of spiritual rights over me when I emerged from that public confession. There was no going back. I was indeed a new creation in Christ. *This* was the manifestation of the power of Jesus in my life. I wish I knew years sooner how the waters would change me— there is something about that simple act of obedience. It was an exchange from the death of the flesh to life in the spirit. The impact is a spiritual shining that pales the celestial stars. The angels see it. And the demons fear it.

You can choose to follow Him or return to your old ways. As for me, I decided I wasn't going back. I wanted everything God had for me. Every day, my life looked less like flesh and more like Spirit. Only God could satiate the hunger and thirst. The hole in my heart was swelling with love for Him. I was inspired by the ministries of Andy Byrd and Sean Feucht, who taught believers the importance of worship and going to places around the world that were spiritually dark to release God's light. They took groups of Christians to dark places and saw atmospheres shift as they worshiped God.

I wanted to know more. I poured over Christian authors like Derek Prince and Francis Frangipane, who taught about deliverance and the battlefield of the mind. I was amazed at missionary biographies like Amy Carmichael and George Mueller, who followed Jesus worldwide and saw miraculous food and healing multiplications. My new passion for God led me from one church to another, searching for water too deep to swim. I wanted that desperate faith where you couldn't touch the bottom.

For a year or so, I would take my guitar and head downtown with a couple of friends. We talked to people going in and out of bars and nightclubs; we bought pizza for homeless people and prayed with them. We were zealous in our faith and wanted to shove Hell back into its abyss by lifting the name of Jesus in worship and outreach. As we walked and prayed one night, I heard a demon hiss out of a woman who silently stood before a psychic shop. I felt a cold, strong wind trying to push us back, but there was no wind that night. I was not scared, and I realized that there was a force I could see, feel, and hear that was a battle against the powers of darkness. The Bible informs us in Ephesians chapter 6 that we do not wrestle against flesh but against rulers, powers of darkness, and spiritual forces of wickedness in heavenly places.

The more I sought Jesus' Kingdom of Light, the more He allowed me to see the power of the dark that He was teaching me to overcome in my life and in others. We shared Jesus every week downtown. We started a homeless church and broke spiritual chains off of people every time. I led worship, and God moved upon hearts. God's contagious love overtook me like waves in the ocean as I shared my testimony with others. The more I gave, the more I wanted to give more. That's how God's Kingdom works. Seeing people take their first-born-again breath was exhilarating.

For the next two years, life became a crescendo of ever-increasing faith. The business grew, and my faith soared. I had a thriving sales business and became self-employed while juggling a public relations business and jazz gigs in a busy schedule. I held a board seat on a peer-advocacy arts council to build a platform for local professionals to stay and serve the region. I felt planted and on my way to success. It seemed my promised land had come. On top of it all, I was planted in a good church and involved in children's ministry and worship. I loved it. Life felt fulfilled in a new way. My sales team was up to fifty women—we packed out my tiny apartment for meetings.

5

NEW BEGINNINGS

I wanted to buy a house. It was time to put down roots. I started looking at homes for sale, feeling rather adulty. Unfortunately, the houses I could afford were rundown and remote. Doubt crept in. *Here we go again*, I thought. *Is this how it's always going to be walking with God?* I wanted an easy road map to life, a straight line up a mountain with a fantastic summit. God's direction seemed more like I was hiking switchbacks in a thick forest. Weeks went by. I prayed.

> *"God, if You want me to buy a house, make it as obvious as a two by four hitting my head."*

I'm glad He didn't whack me on the head. But He did make it that obvious. The same day, I prayed that funny prayer; after looking at three houses that were real duds, I passed an old pale blue house with a sign. I called my realtor and saw the house that afternoon. My heart pounded so hard in my chest. I knew it was for me. Even though it was a foreclosure and needed lots of fixing, I could see its forgotten beauty—glass French doors, original hardwoods, sculpted ceilings. It needed a furnace, new plumbing, and a water heater. The kitchen had no appliances. The walls had graffiti. But something called me to that house—as if it was a lost puppy needing a home, and I had the leash. God sees us like this—we are messy and torn and muddy. Under that mess is a beautiful soul waiting to sparkle in the light. I wanted to help this house sparkle, and I imagined dozens of broken people gathered inside and worshiping God. I told the Lord I would dedicate the house to Him and His purposes, not mine.

After months of phone calls and paperwork, the house was mine. I started remodeling it with a friend. He was a contractor, and I helped however I could, mostly running errands daily for materials. He installed new wiring and plumbing. The rusted-out water heater got thrown out. The driveway was a full dumpster of old plaster and clunky debris.

New things came into the house daily, and it sprang with joy in its resurrected life—just like me. Walls were knocked down, and bathrooms were overhauled. Yellowed vinyl flooring was peeled and scraped to expose beautiful hardwoods. I enjoyed selecting colors for the rooms and painting every inch of two stories with bright, dancing colors.

As I painted the house's entrance foyer moss green with white trim, I had been reading how God instructed the Israelites to inscribe words on the doorposts and gates of their homes. I wrote the Bible verses from Deuteronomy 6 (4-9) in tall painted letters that enveloped the room.

 Hear O Israel, the Lord our God, the Lord is One. Love the Lord your God with all your heart and with all your soul and with all your strength. These words, which I am commanding you today, are to be on your heart. You are to teach them diligently to your children and speak of them when you sit in your house, walk by the way, lie down, and rise. Bind them as a sign on your hand; they are to be frontlets between your eyes. Write them on the doorposts of your house and your gates.

God commanded His people to post this as a reminder on their homes and gates. When I read this, I knew nothing about mezuzahs, the little boxes that Jewish People affix to doorways. I just knew the Bible said to do it, so I painted it in large letters where I would see it in my entry. Meditating on God's words with every passing was a good reminder. It was a marker for a domain, ascribing the acknowledgment of the God of Abraham, Isaac, and Jacob as the God served in that domain. Many Christians don't know much about domains, but the Bible says a lot. Walls around a city, boundary stones being fixed on land, and memorials for physical spaces where God showed up are examples of domains and their importance. I learned spiritual domains were like a welcome mat or stop sign that spirits would heed. I learned about claiming my domain for Jesus. I dedicated the house to the Lord.

I saw these painted words every time I passed the entrance or walked upstairs. I was reminded of everything God was steeping in me like a tea marinating. The atmosphere was charged and palpable to anyone who entered the house. It became a spiritual marker establishing a boundary, similar to the Passover story of applying blood on the door. Doors are entries to domiciles—areas of dominion and authority. What are you allowing to cross your threshold?

There was a time I was talking with a hairdresser who was lamenting about evil presences that bothered her family at her house. Doors slammed when no one was around. She didn't like paranormal activity but said she loved horror movies and getting scared. This is not pleasing to God and opens a door for evil spirits to inhabit a space. Although she claimed to be a Christian, she dug in her heels when I asked her to repent and stop watching that kind of movie that glorified evil. She didn't like the fruit from the tree she had planted. Take an axe to the tree! How can we say Jesus is our Lord and still put our stubborn will above His? When the woman begged me to pray that the evil would leave her home, I told her I wouldn't. I told her, you have a revolving door at your entrance. You can kick them out all you want, but they have legal permission to return. You're wasting your time until you repent and close the doors you opened. Ever hear the expression, 'You can lead a horse to water, but you can't make him drink'? It's our role to help sheep not fall over a cliff if they leave the paddock. But if they keep running to the edge, these are their bad decisions for not heeding warnings.

The Bible is full of clear guidelines. These are there for a reason—to protect us and not to harm us. Parents tell their kids not to run with scissors for their own good. All I could do was encourage her to seek God and humble herself to be willing to change as He spoke to her. Our domains can become defiled if we don't watch our entry points. It is no one's job but ours.

We are called to walk with God and be able to recognize His voice from all others. An infant turns his head toward the voice of his mother or father; a familiar tone causes him to perk up and smile. How do we learn to know God's voice? We become familiar with Him through prayer and reading the Bible. We learn more about who He is, His character, and how He speaks to others in Scripture.

As a baby breathing her first breaths, we grow day by day, each day being a little stronger. Jesus told His disciples to get away from the crowds and get into the boat. There's a pressing forward that is needed to go deep. Finding space to sit in God's presence can sometimes get pushed aside by the busyness of life. But it is more important than taking a breath. Sometimes, it's hard to sit still.

As I settled into the new house, I kept busy with multiple

start-up businesses I launched and found myself reverting to striving in my strength for success. I was gutting and remodeling the house, leading a house ministry, and running like a hamster in a wheel. I needed to tune deeper into God and float in the roll of quiet water.

As Jesus' disciples climbed in the boat, they launched into the same deep they had known for years, but it would be startlingly different when the storm rose upon the sea. They would need to trust Jesus and learn to listen with new ears to keep the boat afloat in a raging storm.

6

LONGING TO MEET

We lean inwards and upwards in our journey of faith in God. There are highs and lows—mountaintops and valleys. We cry to God when we get scared in the storms of life. Does God really hear us? Are we praying into thin air or to an omnipotent Creator who knows us? The Bible says God knows every hair on our heads. He knows when we sit and when we stand.

Psalm 139 describes how God formed us in the innermost place and breathed a specific destiny into each of us. We read that God's thoughts about each one of us are more than the sand on the shore. That's how much He thinks of us and cares about our needs.

Jesus tells us that the Father knows every sparrow and that we are so much more significant to the Father than they are. So if God pays attention to every bird, every flower, every bit of His creation, are you starting to get the picture of how much He loves you? He is always there waiting for you, and He wants us to seek Him out and solicit His presence within our lives. When we seek Him, we find that He is always there.

I had an old wicker brown chair that I kept in the spare

room of the new house. It was shaped like a hamburger patty with a curved back. One day, I remember going into that room and sitting in the chair for a change of scenery away from my busy thoughts. The presence of God fell upon me, knocking me dizzy in a swooning billow of peace. I saw in my mind that I was instantly transported to God's lap; all my worried thoughts faded. It was as if the chair became the transport to transcend me to an immediate connection with God. I was in God's lap every time I sat in that chair. It got to be that I looked forward to sitting in that chair. I called it my God chair.

God is glad when we make space for Him, invite Him in, and let Him teach us real rest. In that rest, He gives us the mind of Christ to silence racing thoughts. After a while, I would glance at the chair and smile, remembering He was and is there waiting to meet with me.

7

CHEESE FOR THAT WHINE

The Lord assured Joshua in the Bible that He would be with him wherever he would go. When we need assurance that God is with us, He is there to steady our wobbling legs. God wanted to set me free from self-reliance. I didn't know how much I needed that freedom. It was during this time that everything fell apart. A new rock bottom crouched around the bend. I ignored my business, believing it would keep thriving without my focus. Once gorged with customers, my sales pipeline became a deflated balloon that lay withered on the ground. I couldn't make a sale to save my life.

I threw myself pity parties, recounting decisions and wondering how I veered off the road of success. Many pastors claimed it was our entitlement.

> *Wasn't the abundant life about health and wealth, fancy cars, and successful careers?*

I had closets full of designer clothing and bucketloads of jewelry. I was young and poised to be somebody. I was a polished professional on the A-list of life and even had God.

What presumption! The underlying root was personal insecurity and pride, trying to find my identity outside of God—and there was no room for that in my vessel if it was to stay afloat.

Self-reliance was the water that overflowed and shook the boat. Through trial, I learned that I'm not a dependable bail and anchor; God is the only one to Whom we can safely anchor.

> *My definition of success was not congruent with who God wanted me to be.*

His idea of beauty and success was a quiet and peaceful confidence rooted in Him where the Spirit pours like oil from the inside out, not from the outside. I wasn't there by a long shot, and I pleaded with God and friends for answers. Friends visited and prayed, offering stories of miracles and testimonies.

My faith needed oxygen. I didn't know what to do. And I didn't realize that season would last two long years.

I felt like Job from the Bible when he lost everything. I was reminded of Joseph, who had been thrown into a pit.

THE FIRST LAYER of healing was about to commence. Months earlier, when I finished painting every room of my new house and sat back to admire my work, I exclaimed to my friends that I would never again paint a home. Fun as it was, it was backbreaking work.

Jesus warned about the weight of vows—that when we say "I will" or "I won't," we put our wills above God's. There is conflict when someone else, God, is supposed to sit on our heart's throne. What servant tells his master he won't do something? How can we flippantly say such things when we do not know what might be required?

Now listen, you who say, 'Today or tomorrow we will go to this or that city, spend a year there, carry on business and make money.' Why, you do not even know what will happen tomorrow. What is your life? You are a mist that appears for a little while and then vanishes. Instead, you should say, 'If it is the Lord's will, we will do this or that.' (James 4:13-15)

During this rough patch, I reached a new low when I contacted friends to offer help babysitting or any odd job.

I couldn't buy food. I couldn't pay the mortgage. I couldn't put gas in the car. I think I started biting my nails again.

Then, a friend called and asked if I could paint her bathroom. If so, could I paint her bathroom? I reluctantly agreed with a heavy sigh, hating the idea. Tears ran down my cheeks as I taped and painted around the toilet and tub. I had to pay the bills, but pride was at stake.

After painting the bathroom, she asked me to paint the entire basement. As a newlywed, she recently moved into her husband's house, which needed a facelift. I painted day after day, blowing my nose from crying.

When that room was finished, she asked me to stay on because it would mean so much to her if I could paint the outdated kitchen. With each stroke of paint, that room burst to life, but I was angry that God had menial labor for me to do. I sank from hosting lavish jewelry parties to painting someone's bathroom in sweatpants.

I painted the living room, followed by the long hallway and stairwell, and weeks passed. I cried less after another three rooms were done, and I resigned myself to this new station in life. I went home every night and fell into bed exhausted.

At the end of it all, I had painted every room of her house, the same number of rooms as mine. God was breaking my vow, one room at a time. Do you remember when Peter denied Jesus three times, and after the resurrection, Jesus asked Peter three times if he loved Him and to feed His sheep? The power of our words is real. God takes us seriously and doesn't like when we put our will above His.

It was getting close to the mortgage due date. I sat home one night covered in paint and opened my bleak checkbook. I was still five hundred dollars short. Alone at my table, I cried out to God.

> "You know I'm doing all I can. I am still short five hundred dollars. Please help."

As soon as I prayed, an unusual peace came upon me. I closed the checkbook and felt strangely serene. Was it the paint fumes from the long day, or was this the presence of God? I was at the end of myself. I slept soundly that night. I had no idea how to pay the bill, but I knew I had done all I could.

It wasn't enough that I had Jesus in my heart. I had to get it in my heart that He held me in His heart. I had to overcome unworthiness masked in pride.

The following day, I went to the house to paint. I wasn't finished with a few rooms and had another week of painting. I asked my friend if there was any way she could pay me more than the agreed-upon hourly rate and that I was having trouble making ends meet. She was empathetic but said it was a fixed budget and there was no wiggle room. I nodded sadly.

Then, in the moment of quiet pause, before I stood up to start painting, my understanding of God's goodness shifted forever.

She reached into her pocket. Putting a small white envelope in my hand, she told me the Lord told her to give it to me as a gift. Inside the envelope was a check, and it was written for precisely five hundred dollars. No one heard my prayer but God. No one knew my need but God.

I burst into tears and told her the story, causing her to cry and laugh with me.

My efforts scraping by were not rooted in trusting God, and He taught me that morning that He *does* hear my prayers and genuinely cares. Self-reliance had to be crushed. I learned that He heard, answered, and comforted me as I walked that bumpy road of faith.

He was proving to me that He was a good Father, teaching me and helping me to walk. I marveled that someone else could hear so specifically from God and respond with such generous obedience. No one overheard my prayer; only God knew.

I had been scraping by with a morsel of faith and a bucket of self-determination. I needed to be broken of pride. That was what God was doing. He was very kind to me.

I couldn't believe God would ask someone to give that much, and I couldn't believe she was willing to obey. I had a lot to learn about God. That day, I began a walk of quiet confidence, knowing God would always meet my needs. I just had to trust Him. I received grace and favor through the fires of a desperate petition, like a keyboard sustaining an eternal note that rang, "I've got you, and I am with you."

8

BAPTIZED IN FIRE

I hosted worship and prayer gatherings at my house. Friends and strangers would come and have encounters with God. I loved that, but I loved the time I sat alone with my guitar and God more. During one of these times, worshiping God alone, my words became indecipherable utterings of sound—the room was empty—just me and my dog. I paused, wondering where those syllables were from, then resumed singing. I had heard of speaking in tongues, but it was foreign to me, so I called my uncle.

"This is one of God's gifts," my uncle assured me, telling me not to be afraid.

I went back to worship and let the strange sounds forth. I discovered a new muscle in my spiritual body and was flexing for the first time. I felt I was dictating shorthand to God but couldn't understand what I was saying. The language evolved from indecipherable phonetics to actual phrases and words in other languages, including Chinese, Hebrew, and Coptic Egyptian. When a specific phrase turned often, I googled it phonetically, only to discover obsolete ancient languages.

Once in church, we watched a film clip about Romanian

missionaries, and my spirit jumped because I recognized that language from praying in the Spirit.

When we speak in tongues, we release God's voice through ours, bringing fruit from seeds we do not realize we carry. Paul prayed for all believers to desire this gift earnestly and to pray in both Spirit and mind. This is all possible with God. As we pray in the Spirit, the Spirit prompts us to pray in our minds.

> *In the first sputterings of this new gift, I imagined the image of an old rusty faucet tap that sat too long. The pump needed priming—the air had to clear for the water to gush out.*

We push past the fear of sounding strange, and the pump is primed. We need the Holy Spirit today more than ever, interceding through and for us. It's also helpful to pray in the Spirit for people specifically and intercede while avoiding the sin of gossip or meddling in their personal affairs.

A well of living water is waiting to burst forth from every believer. We invite God to renew our spirits by the breath of His Spirit so He can commission us to do His will. Jesus told His disciples,

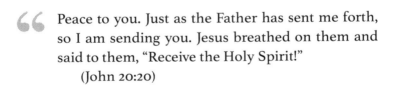

> Peace to you. Just as the Father has sent me forth, so I am sending you. Jesus breathed on them and said to them, "Receive the Holy Spirit!"
> (John 20:20)

God created us to walk with Him. Ephesians 1:3-6 says God has blessed us with every spiritual blessing in the heavenly places in Christ. We submit ourselves to God. Even though we walk here on the earth in worshipful submission to God, we ascend into Heaven and speak directly with God when we speak in a spiritual language. The prayers bypass the enemy, who cannot decipher what God's Spirit within us is speaking to the atmosphere through us and to the Father. It is a powerful weapon that is needed today more than ever.

Jesus said it was better that He go to the Father so that we would have the Holy Spirit's filling. This is huge. Imagine having Jesus walk in the resurrected flesh for two millennia or having the Holy Spirit fill us to do more extraordinary things in Jesus' name. This was the better option, Jesus told His followers.

There would not be enough space in all of Earth to contain the books that could be written because we would do them in His name and power. Holy Spirit intercedes in a way our limited minds do not fathom. Sometimes, God gives the interpretation, or He may quicken us to pray for a specific situation.

Praying for someone or something in the Spirit is powerful; it pushes past our human limitations and aligns God's Spirit in us to bear witness in prayer with God Himself, the witness of two, and to bypass any interference from the Kingdom of darkness.

9

GOOD FATHER

Sometimes, we have the wrong idea of who God is as a Father. Maybe you grew up without a dad, or your relationship with your father wasn't good. We project these emotions to God, thinking He is angry with us, a strict disciplinarian, or uninvolved. God is a compassionate father who is gentle in love. He wants to be involved and active in your life, and He isn't a tyrant. Shifting how we think about God makes a difference in how we relate to Him. His love is extravagant, and His mercy is limitless. There are rules for good behavior in His family, but He quickly forgives when we mess up.

Through Jesus, we have access to the Father, and the formality that was once in place is now replaced with an invitation to come boldly to His presence. We are a family, and there is love in the house. Children can play freely in their homes. They can wander from the formal foyer to the relaxed family room. They can stretch out on the sofa and get a snack from the refrigerator if hungry. Wouldn't it be weird to think kids couldn't be at ease in their house?

When we invite Jesus into our hearts, God adopts us as His children in His family. We don't have to beg for food when we sit for dinner. Wouldn't it be weird if your parents refused to give you bread and said you weren't worthy of a morsel?

The Bible says an earthly father gives good things to his children. How much *more* does God do for His children?

> If you then, being evil, know how to give good gifts to your children, how much more will your heavenly Father give good things to those who ask Him. (Matthew 7:11)

If you want a second helping of potatoes at dinner, in a typical family, you would ask, "More, please," and expect someone to pass you the dish.

> What father, if his son asks for a fish, will give him a snake instead? If he asks for an egg, will he give him a scorpion? If you, being evil, know how to give good gifts to your children, how much more will your heavenly Father give to those who ask Him. (Luke 11:11-13)

Sadly, some Christians do not know that God is a good and loving father. Religion teaches man-made governance systems that are formal and rigid, but God's way is familial and loving. Religion tells us to beg, kneel, and plead; our relationship with the Father invites us to dance, play, and be loved by Papa God.

Walking in faith simply requires us to desire more of God and what pleases our Father. Because we love Him, we want to live holy lives. We are not beaten by a whip for failing but taken by the hand and encouraged to get up and try walking again, like a toddler that tumbles. What parent yells when their small child stumbles? They help and encourage them. It is time to push past the iron gates erected by religious systems so we can climb into Daddy's lap, lean on His chest, and connect with the source of our lives.

Religion impedes, limiting the flow of God's extravagant love.

God wants a family. There is order and function within the family, but it is a different mode of operation from what religion suggests. Religion and relationships are on opposite ends of the seesaw. Religion is a flag posted on a previous act of God to erect a structure to identify and classify God. But God is still moving today.

The church age is over.

God is calling us to dwell with Him and Him in us. Jesus, the Son of God, became a man. He came to Earth and became a Son of Man so that we, who are Sons of Man, could become Sons of God. This goes beyond what churches say, and it's time to step into our true identities. *We* are the living stones that make up the church building. It is not made of stone or concrete. We *are* the church, walking and moving! God says He will do new things, as much of the Bible demonstrates. How can we put a period where there is a dot dot dot?

We belong to the family of God. He is the perfect father, giving His children dependable protection, provision, and correction. While He has rules to follow, they are for our safety and benefit, not our resentment. His children are to be joyful and free. His children can climb in the trees dressed in drapery like the kids on Sound of Music. They do not have to march around in military clothes and answer to military whistles. His children come freely to the table; they do not beg for crumbs. His children are secure because they know Father is good.

BECAUSE WE HAVE a Father who delights and is involved in the lives of all His children.

10

JULIA

I was growing in my walk as a follower of Jesus. I read the Bible, learning to hear God's voice. I prayed, worshiped, and shared Jesus with fire and joy. I felt pretty good about the healing layers I had worked through.

But there were still deep hurts in my heart from the past that weren't healed. I had painful memories and traumas from my past; I wanted complete healing and needed help to get freedom. I was learning a lot from Biblical teachers and authors such as Derek Prince and Mark Virkler—I realized the powers of Hell still had legal ground to afflict me in areas where I wasn't set free. I heard about a healing workshop for women that a nearby church offered, so I signed up. I was scared to expose unhealed areas of my soul but desperate to be free.

I walked into the classroom to see twenty twitching women awkwardly standing. One woman's face made my skin crawl—I saw a putrid green face superimposed on hers and something like a grayish shadow that cast her skin color to look as if it was behind a shroud of smoke. I glanced around, but no one else seemed to see it. The instructor told us to form a circle. The woman stood next to me, her face morphing like a hologram with shifting faces. The instructor told the group to take hands to pray. The woman, Julia, grabbed my hand. I prayed. Silently, I bound the Spirit of fear that was coming against me; I asked the Holy Spirit to push back the darkness from Julia. Electricity shot through my hand to hers, and she shook violently.

After a while, I couldn't handle the meeting and all the critters in the room. I muttered an excuse for forgetting a prior commitment and flung myself out the back door. Driving home, I argued with myself and told myself I wasn't as bad as the people in that room and didn't need that class. But deep down, I knew my heart needed healing, and God loved me enough to see it through.

As we journey with Jesus, we allow space for Him to open doors in our souls and memories that we kept locked so He can set us free. Neil Andersen's books helped me to learn how to forgive and release others from my judgment, including myself. Derek Prince wrote many books that helped me along my journey to healing with God. God's light continuously expels darkness.

LIFE IS NOT A STRAIGHT LINE; our response to life's ups and downs shapes our character. Will we trust? Will we forgive? Will we hope when hope seems lost? With every high and low, God builds for us a crown. He uses what the enemy intended to harm for our benefit. Tests become testimonies. Messes become messages. What we think of as failure, God uses to grow us in wisdom and maturity through Him. A crown is made when you connect the dots of the highs and lows. The dots brought together represent our promised reward, a priceless and beautiful crown testifying of every victory in battle.

With our eyes on Jesus, we press forward from the low valley toward the next waiting mountaintop.

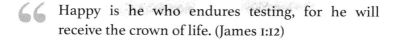 Happy is he who endures testing, for he will receive the crown of life. (James 1:12)

11

THE GIFT OF BROKENNESS

On Wednesday nights, I went to a tiny church in a few towns over for quaint but anointed worship. While the music wasn't my style, with pipe organs, banjos, and white-haired worshippers, the Presence of God was strong in that modest chapel.

Although business failed me, God was teaching me that He never did. He was all I had. After years of sitting on the comfy executive side of Boardroom tables, the tables had turned. I went from helping the down-and-outs through administrative efforts to becoming one, from enjoying $200 plate fundraisers to grabbing leftover bread thrown in black trash bags on the floor of the city mission.

The government gave me a small box of canned food and two rolls of toilet paper every month. For that, I had to bring three pieces of personal identity and mail to redeem food I wouldn't have bought in a store. One day, I was in line for my food box when I saw a frail elderly man on crutches getting yelled at and turned away because he did not bring proof of his identity. I saw him explain that he had taken the city bus for one hour with the help of his daughter and didn't even have money to take the bus home. I cried for a long time that night. My heart broke for that man and the callousness of a system that was not compassionate to the hurting.

God was teaching me to trust in Him and share His heart for this world's brokenness. The more challenging things became, the more I ran to God's arms to worship Him; I had nothing to hold onto but God. I must remind myself of that now when life can seem comfortable. I want always to have that heart that runs to God.

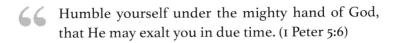

Humble yourself under the mighty hand of God, that He may exalt you in due time. (1 Peter 5:6)

God was breaking my heart more for the poor than myself, and I saw many hurting people. I saw why Jesus had so much compassion. I broke bread with the poor and invited them to my house for worship gatherings. I let them stay in the house while I ran errands, showing them dignity withheld by others. A friend thought I was crazy for trusting homeless people in my home when I wasn't there, but I had nothing of concerning value and saw more value in them. They were just as astounded at my trust, and I watched them bloom to life from that trust.

I was on God's surgical table during this today, and something beautiful was happening. He cut my pride like a cancerous cell, followed by a healing season of tremendous brokenness. He filled me with supernatural love. My credentials no longer mattered—they did not define me any longer. I was a human being with a heart that desperately needed an infusion to replace the pride masked as confidence. I needed to build my identity upon the unshakable rock: Jesus, who would be my steady, unwavering foundation in every storm. In my utmost dependence on God, when I reached the end of myself, He brought me into a new layer of faith for me to emerge like a tiny worm from a protective cocoon.

The Gift of Brokenness

EVERY WEDNESDAY NIGHT, the church I went to had a food pantry, and they loaded my trunk with boxes of things they would throw away. I was getting the waste from the waste and turning it into something beautiful. Isn't that what God does with us? I filled my car with half-spoiled apples, mushy tomatoes, and flattened strawberries. I learned ways to salvage what I could, and I loved every minute of it, churning out gallons of applesauce, marinara, and baked treats. My kitchen had found its purpose, and I carried homemade sauce and loaves of banana bread with me on my morning dog walks, praying to see who I could bless.

There was a frail elderly man who lived around the block, homebound and sick. I started visiting, listening to his stories, and praying for him. We talked in his living room, where he lived out of one chair and a TV tray. Those visits became the highlight of my week. The more I gave away what little I had, the more God blessed me. The less I had, the more generous I became.

Part of what God is drawing us toward is the maturing that comes from the trials and pitfalls that come our way. If everything was rosy and easy, where would we be? Would we see His miraculous display? It is in the night seasons that the light burns brightest. Strangely, the poorest season of my life has been my most prosperous season with God.

> When you have nothing but God,
> you realize you need nothing but God.

Would we seek Him first or wallow in our pity and worry? Could we step out and serve others, no matter how bleak our cupboards might be? God sent me surprises weekly—a mysterious envelope of hundreds of dollars was pushed under my front door. Thousands of dollars were wadded up and anonymously left for me. The bills were getting paid, but much more than that— I had the peace of God. I learned to trust God for all my needs and that He cared. A song returned to my heart like a robin after winter.

It is easy to forget the goodness of God in our lives. We move forward so fast that we can forget the gifts along the way, the memorial stones in our hearts of when he meets us with a holy kiss. I sometimes miss those days of hardship, making sauces and loaves because the constant conversation with God was so holy and beautiful. He constantly comforted me. Even if I didn't enjoy eating at soup kitchens or painting houses, I learned to trust Him. My path was becoming prosperous because I was walking with God. I was comforted in distress and affliction as He led me in paths of righteousness for His Name's sake, as it is written in Psalm 23. He was renewing my spirit and breaking me from myself, taking the hard clay I was and softening it. I was learning to believe I was loved by the Most High and could look up at the heavens and see all the spiritual blessings coming my way. They were much richer than material blessings. Trusting God when things don't make sense is how we grow as His children.

When we relinquish our rights to ourselves, we permit God to rearrange stuff so our hearts can become healed, pure, and whole. That's much more important than money or comfort or material things. Strip them all away, and you have just you— skin and bones and a heart and soul, which the Father is digging deep to get to. This is His anthem of love for us, a song He sings over us until it seeps into the very marrow of our bones. When we are saturated, we respond with every fiber and cell singing back to Him with thanksgiving from an overflowing heart. It no longer matters if we are in prison like Paul or a pit like Joseph. No matter what we are going through, our Father knows every hair on our heads and cares about us. We are unshakable when our identity is secure because we know who we are. We can feel His love all around us.

Slowing down, we find God's peace that surpasses understanding, and our spirit can breathe deeper and more confidently, knowing it is not up to us to fix every little thing because there is a God who loves us. What a comfort, a strange understanding that we are all connected by His Spirit, and each is part of His heart. This is how God's Kingdom is: sharing our blessings and submitting our hearts, wills, and dreams to the Lordship of God.

12

THE RETURN OF JULIA

One night, sometime later, my friend Ivan wanted to bring a new guest to my house to worship that night. When I opened my door, Julia was standing in my doorway. She was the woman from the deliverance meeting shaken violently by evil spirits, the one I wanted to get away from. I froze and gasped. *This* was his guest? How could I let that hideous demon into my house? It was bad enough I had to hold her hand in prayer. I took my friend Sam into the kitchen.

"That's the woman I told you about!"

Sam calmed me down, telling me to trust God (a common theme I was working on). I picked up my guitar and led us all in worship, deciding I would not engage with Julia. I would focus all my attention on God. Worship calmed my nerves and rebuked fear because my focus was shifted entirely to Jesus, who is King over all. Every spirit must submit to His Name.

After singing a few songs, with my closed eyes in worship, I felt a shift and opened my eyes to glance around the room. Sam, Ivan, and Luis were praying for Julia, and I watched as

God was getting that hideous green demon out of her—right there in my living room! I watched it flee from her body as my friends huddled around her to cast it out in prayer. She was crying, her arms held high, declaring her love for Jesus and repenting out loud as my friends ministered to her. God's holy presence and angels overtook my home, and I burst into exuberant throne-room worship in the radiant presence of God. Julia's eyes became radiant without that green vapory smog from Hell. We all enjoyed a long evening of worship, prayer, and joy for what God had done. After many hugs late into the night, they all said goodbye and left. Suddenly, I was alone. In a moment, I was gripped with fear. *Oh my goodness, that hideous thing is in my house now.* I phoned my friends for prayer. They came rushing over. I shared my fears.

"My house is not clean. How can I sleep here? That thing is lurking here, I know it."

We prayed over the house, and peace was restored. I learned the importance of anointing one's home, praying through it, and kicking any foul thing out in Jesus' name. Just like our bodies need washing, so do our things, especially when serving the Lord in deliverance ministry, which we are all supposed to do. Cockroaches are gross, but they must be crushed. I learned how to pray and anoint my house and possessions in Jesus' name. When I didn't have peace about something, I would ask God what I was to do. I also learned the importance of staking property lines to take legal authority in the spirit realm. It was like putting a 'no trespassing' sign in the spirit, with implications for rule-breakers.

A year later, Julia started attending our worship in the city park. She was free. Before her freedom in Jesus, she suffered sexual abuse, incest, drugs, depression, and bipolar schizophrenia. All that Hell had to leave her when she gave herself to Jesus and invited Him in to set her free. Isn't God wonderful? She was a new creation in Christ. I was healed. My faith grew. My home was spiritually clean.

∼

AND I WAS NO LONGER afraid.

13

HEART REDEMPTION

Freedom is the open road on the other side of the bridge of forgiveness. When we harbor unforgiveness, we grab God's gavel of justice and cruelly demand vengeance for others and clemency for ourselves. The balance is skewed as our imperfections become mere peccadillos in our eyes, and we forget what we have done that has been forgiven. Planks and specks get easily mixed up, depending on the storyteller.

Remember with humility the great lengths God took to rescue you. Even if the heart does not want to forgive, the commandment stands fast, and by obeying God and extending forgiveness, the heart eventually follows. Our plea should be one of mercy, as Jesus cried from the cross,

 "Father, forgive them, for they know not what they do."

No person is too far that God cannot reach and rescue. I once spoke to a crowd of women at a church retreat, and the theme was to expose darkness to God's light. I addressed sexual

sins and the shame attached, including abortion, rape, and abuse. God wants all things out of the shadows so that His love and mercy can bring restoration to both perpetrators and victims.

I asked one hundred women in that room to stand to their feet if they had suffered sexual abuse or abortion. More than fifty women stood up. Everyone is affected by sin. No one but Jesus has walked in undefiled purity their entire life. Women at that retreat were freed from the enemy's chains when God's light shone in the hidden closets of shame. No one is without sin. *All* are within the reach of God's arm for complete forgiveness.

We must forgive others with the same desperate plea to God for His mercy. Even if they hurt us, we are commanded to forgive. It doesn't excuse sin but transfers all judgment to God.

Jesus addressed this in a parable. In Matthew 18:32, a man was forgiven an outstanding debt by his master but then screamed at his servant, who owed him a small amount. Jesus warned,

 This is how my heavenly Father will treat you unless you forgive from your heart.

God has forgiven us an outstanding debt and bestowed upon us eternal life. Peter asked Jesus, "Master, how often shall I forgive my brother? Up to seven times?"

Jesus said, "No, not up to seven times, I tell you, but seventy times seven."

As long as we live, we must forgive.

MANY BELIEVERS STRUGGLE TO relate to the woman who broke her alabaster jar over Jesus' feet, washing him with her tears.

She knew she was forgiven much. The jar contained her lifetime savings, probably a dowry worth over thirty thousand dollars. Some disciples mocked, saying, "Does the Master know who that is touching Him?" Jesus said in Luke 7:36,

 "Her sins, which are many, are forgiven, for she loved much. But the one who is forgiven little loves little."

Reflecting on my shaky beginnings before I walked with Jesus, I am grateful Jesus saved me.

Forgiveness is the magnet that draws broken pieces together. No matter how serious the offense, relinquish everything to God's hands.

SINCE I WAS A LITTLE GIRL, I had crushes on boys, from little Robbie in kindergarten, who was my secret prince until he peed his pants in the cafeteria, losing his knightly luster, to innocent preteen crushes with swapped handwritten notes on blue-lined school paper. It is natural to have these childlike infatuations as girls and boys learn to be friends. As I got older, I sought value through relationships, leading to bad decisions. God cares about the wounded deserts in your heart that He wants to water. Redemption is for wholeness, with no part unhealed. I had carried scars within my heart for years, and it was time for God to bring redemption for my heart to be fertile soil once again.

I met a man who swept me off my feet when I was twenty. He had returned from studying art in Florence, Italy, and opened the world to me, living larger than life. We rode his motorcycle, and my knees knocked with adrenaline. We painted the town and had a whirlwind relationship. When the romance ended, he left me with a broken heart. I lost both faith in men and respect for myself. The years following were a downward spiral until Jesus saved me. I forgot about him but continued to make bad decisions for years, coming from a place of deep hurt in my heart. God wanted to take an ax to the tree of that hurt.

Seventeen years later, God spoke to me to reach out to him. I argued with God about the insanity of trying to find someone after so long—I brashly told God I would spend only five minutes online to find him on Google, and that was that. If God wanted us to connect, it would happen. Interestingly, I found him in one minute because that's how God works sometimes. Brian called me on the phone within the hour, as incredulous as I was at this unexpected reunion.

Brian and I fell into a rhythm of long-lost friends catching up. He'd become a world-famous architect and designed award-winning buildings in London and Philadelphia. I shared how I lived in Barcelona, Seattle, and New York, with jazz, public relations, and consulting careers. We were both astounded.

"Have you ever married?" he asked me.

"No, you?"

"No."

Then God came into the conversation. I laughed because I did not want to sound foolish by saying God prompted me to reach out. As we talked, I admitted that the real reason I'd messaged him was a prompt of the Lord. I spilled out my journey with God, relieved to be honest. Brian listened intently, and when the call ended, he exclaimed he'd love to meet me for coffee as soon as possible, as we only lived two hours away. We hung up, both of us elated and surprised.

Ten minutes later, my phone rang, and it was Brian, with a serious tone. He told me he wanted to tell me something he had never told anyone until recently about a girl in Italy he dated before he met me and how she got pregnant, aborted twins, went nuts, shaved her head, and lived as a homeless person. He found her wandering the streets when he returned to Italy to propose marriage to her with a ring in hand. Our relationship followed on the heels of his deep hurt.

"Then, I met you and you were wonderful, amazing. And I know I treated you awful."

I gulped with raw emotions, listening to his confession and remembering the bad memories of his callousness toward me.

"I am so sorry I hurt you and took my pain out on you. You deserved so much better."

Emotions flooded back as I remembered how he hardened my heart with his behavior toward me. We both started crying.

"Why don't we both pray together and ask God to forgive us both?" I suggested.

As we prayed, God's love rushed in. He thanked me for forgiving him. We planned to meet in the coming weeks. When I hung up the phone, I laughed, cried, and felt freedom sweep over me like a tsunami. The latent hatred I'd carried for years was gone. My heart empathized for all the men who hurt me, and I realized they all had stories. Hurts broke off from me like dead branches from a tree that wanted to live. The ax swung.

I walked on clouds. I was positive God was reconciling us. It was the perfect love story—guy and girl unredeemed in sin, and set free decades later through Jesus. I had a permanent smile on my face.

Two weeks later, my phone rang. Brian's father told me he had never stopped talking excitedly about me since our call and was excited to see me again, talking about marriage to his folks. Then he said Brian was in the hospital, and it didn't look good, so if I wanted to visit, I should get there immediately.

I left the house immediately and drove one hundred miles to the hospital with uncombed hair and no makeup. When I got to his side and called his name, his eyes lit up with a smile.

Brian was in pre-coma. He squeezed my hand and wouldn't let go. I sat for hours, talking to him about Jesus and miracles in my life, holding nothing back. He took everything in, holding my hand tightly. I told him how good Jesus is.

I told him how our prayer two weeks ago set me free. His eyes locked on mine, searching, wanting desperately to speak. We had that long conversation just two weeks earlier, and he didn't know he was ill—how quickly things can change. For five hours, I prayed over him, holding him close. When I told a hospital nurse we had just reconnected after seventeen years, she replied that patients reach out to make amends before they die.

"No", I told her. "He didn't reach out to me. I reached out to him because the Lord told me to."

The next day, two new nurses, Faith and Joy, showed up to attend to him. After that week they disappeared, and the hospital had no record of them.

I thought about the preciousness of second chances and God's kindness in healing our hearts. When I went home the next morning, I fasted and prayed for the next four days without sleep. After I left, Brian lifted his arms and called out the only word he had spoken all week—Jesus! I discovered he had not given his heart to Jesus until then, despite being raised in a born-again Christian home.

"You're the reason he finally did," his dad told me.

I thought about how God uses surprise people to reach the center of one's heart; it's not always who we expect. But it's exactly how God intended because He knows who can touch that delicate place of the heart.

After four days of fasting and crying to the Lord, I started to look like a specter with no sleep and intense travail in the Spirit for his life. I begged God to heal him. I pleaded with God to have mercy. On the fourth day, my room became enveloped with a resounding presence, and someone stood behind me.

Two arms encircled my waist and rocked me for a long, silent time. It was the purest ethereal love. I rested my head back. Suddenly, two toddler boys with black curl ringlets bobbing around their faces chased each other in my foyer, giggling. I watched this surreal scene and smiled. They looked like little Mediterranean princes with olive complexions, full of joy. I watched them running in circles, arms around my waist the entire time. My grief melted away; the fatigue vanished. The absolute pureness of love surrounded me. Then, slowly, ever so slowly, everything faded, and I was standing alone again with the warmth on my waist where two arms held me.

My phone rang. His father called to say Brian just passed peacefully. The following week after his funeral, I planted a rose bush as a reminder of God's love—beauty from thorns, just like a rose. I wanted a different ending to the story and grieved, but God knew it was more important that Brian receive salvation and that I receive heart healing. How extravagant is God's love. A month earlier, I hadn't thought of Brian for years, and he didn't know he was sick.

If I had not stepped into the uncomfortable and awkward place of obedience to God's prompting to reach out, I might still harbor pain from past hurts, and Brian might not have received critical salvation.

God knows exactly what we need if we will turn our ears to Him.

> *Broken and frayed threads can create the prettiest tapestries with colors of real redemption. Beauty always comes from the ashes of forgiveness.*

A more challenging task can be in forgiving ourselves. If God can forgive us our sins, shouldn't we? Is our judgment higher than God's? Is it not true that love keeps no record of wrongs? *Do we truly believe we buried that sucker in a watery grave?* Do not allow that corpse to float back to the water's surface. The old man is buried in Christ, and a new man lives in his place. God wants you to believe that truth, that you are forgiven fully, and you are expected to dole out the exact measure to others and yourself. Let God heal your heart in His perfect love. Your heart is the most beautiful real estate on the earth, and God is bent on ploughing the lumps and planting good seeds. Redemption can bring forth the most exquisite flower. Despite thorns, it lifts a radiant bloom. It is the symbol of romantic love. Its oil is the most expensive oil you can buy. And the bestower of its flower drinks in the rose's fragrance, which is a beautiful offering.

We trust God to lead us to complete healing, extravagant freedom, and unmerited favor.

~

THAT'S how much He loves us.

14

UNDER HIS WING

God assembles the broken pieces when we break from ourselves to make a beautiful masterpiece. We become fashioned more like Jesus. I was learning to lean on God even when I didn't understand what He was doing. A mother hen collects her chicks under her wing to protect them. In that safe place, she raises them. In Psalm 139, David marveled that God knows every little detail about every person, even when they sit and stand. Jesus taught that God cares for every little sparrow. Although I often felt like a bird afraid to jump off a branch to test its wings, the call of Jesus is to follow Him on the lilting winds of His grace and not to stand frozen in fear on a stoic branch.

We are called to trust God. A great world exists, and we have wings to fly. Let God cradle you in His hand and give you breadcrumbs from His table. In His care, your racing heartbeat slows and stressed limbs unfurl. Soon, you doze in contentment. When you wake, you happily trot off from His open hand, knowing He will care for you. May our lives be so entwined with the Father that we live from this place of dependence and trust—rest and refreshment.

Jesus' yoke is light and easy. If things feel burdensome, it is because we carry what we are not meant to. I worked as hard as possible, but it was no longer with a striving spirit. My business dried up, and I struggled to pay the bills, but my heart fell more in love with God. When things seem to be going well, we don't always regard God because we can think we accomplished it by ourselves. It's when we need wind in our sails that we look up.

There was a Bible verse I clung to during that long tunnel of financial desperation.

> Cast all your cares on the Lord, BEE-cause He cares for you. (1 Peter 5:7)

It was a page torn from a kid's coloring book. There was a bumblebee, a sticker of a cast on a broken leg, and butterflies drawn in crayon. I smiled at it every morning as I padded downstairs to the kitchen in slippers to make coffee.

I was learning to stand my ground, resist the enemy, and watch him flee as I stood on God's promises. I was learning to cast all my cares on God. The enemy tried to remind me of my past, but I stood on the Scriptures and declared my new identity in Jesus.

The more challenging things got, the more I rushed into God's arms to worship Him; I had nothing but Him. When times get comfortable, we need to remember the lean times. I worked to make ends meet. What I needed to lose was stubborn self-reliance. The Bible tells us when we are weak, God is strong. As I got this into my head, things got easier. I told God my needs and started believing He would care for me. I recorded every need God met in a notebook called 'Blessings.' The pages were filled with small and simple blessings. Maybe I didn't have enough money to fill my gas tank, but I could be thankful for ten dollars for gas or a hot cup of coffee. As the months passed, my faith soared, and something lifted from inside me. I knew my heart was healed. It wasn't a specific moment; it was like a caterpillar poking through a cocoon and seeing that the world had not ended but was just about to begin.

Although there are depths to God we do not comprehend, the Bible assures us not to be afraid. Isn't it interesting that this command is mentioned three hundred and sixty-five days in the Bible? One could infer that we are encouraged to walk in faith every day. Fear is not from God, so we must reject it. God watches over His children with the attention of a mother hen with her chicks. He cares about you and me. Even when things don't make sense, we trust Him and press into Him for direction. In the Bible, Psalm 91 assures the reader that God protects His children and instructs them to stay close to Him like a chick with its mother. He will watch over us. We must have faith like children, trust His leading, and abide closely by Him.

Like an eagle with her babies, the chick depends entirely on its mother for survival. Faith and trust cover us. We should be clinging close enough to God to feel His Spirit upon us like breath. He is our safe refuge. The more we abide with God, the more we will grow as sons and daughters of God. We run when we run *with* Him. We soar when we soar *with* Him.

I HIKED with my dog one snowy morning in a winter wonderland of snow-kissed evergreens. The branches bowed with snow weight, and my feet sank with each step. Duncan ran and brushed tree branches, the snow fluttering against the backdrop of the sun. I was undone by the majesty of creation and lifted my arms in praise. I danced alone in the snowy tundra with my face toward the big blue sky. An enormous deer bounded across the path before me, sending snow flurrying as his antlers brushed the trees. The moment was holy; I knew God was there.

The Bible tells us the Lord quiets us with His love and dances over us with singing. As I worshiped God in the lush white landscape, the atmosphere shifted with the glory of Heaven.

I was hungry for more of God. I wanted to step into the deep end of the swimming pool where my feet couldn't touch the bottom. I found an unexpected freedom in not knowing where God would lead me. In the midst of poverty, I learned how rich I truly was.

AND I WAS surprised that I preferred depending on God rather than myself.

15

TWO THINGS IN MY HANDS

I kept wondering about the story in the Bible where the rich young man asked Jesus what more he needed to do. When Jesus told him to sell everything and follow me, the man sadly walked away. I wondered repeatedly, *What more is there to gain by letting everything go and following Jesus?*

Whatever it was, I wanted as much and everything as Jesus had to give. I was tired of working to pay for stuff I didn't need or want. The American dream had lost its luster, and everything I had collected only weighed me down.

I felt like a turtle with a heavy shell on its back, trudging through life, wanting to ditch the shell and run free. My turtle shell was the house I'd worked so hard to renovate and restore, dedicated to the Lord's service. Was He asking me to give it up after just getting it? I promised the Lord I would use it for Him and was faithful. But the bills were a struggle, and work wasn't dependable. Plus, it was nearly the end of the school year, and my temporary job as a substitute teacher would soon end. I prayed about what God might be preparing me for, feeling an unexpected tug on my heart for world missions. Many of my friends went in that direction. I applauded them, but it wasn't for me.

And yet, I wanted more.

I wrestled with the budding idea of going into world missions. But I didn't know what I would do with the house and with my dog. I had a loyal companion for a decade: my dog Duncan, an energetic chocolate lab. He brought joy to my life, swimming with otters in Puget Sound, chasing woodchucks on the banks of the Hudson River, hunting, hiking, and kayaking in whitewater with me. He was an avid explorer, just like me. I brought him with me as a companion to the old and infirm at senior homes and children's hospitals, in worship gatherings where strangers would pet him, and we'd get to talking about Jesus. When I played guitar, Duncan sat at the feet of his mistress as a loyal friend. He was a riot and a mischief; at eleven years of age, he still had many dog years ahead. Rehousing him was out of the question, and if I went overseas for missions, I'd have to find someone to take care of him for months.

I prayed.

> *"Lord, I have these two things in my hands—*
> *my house and my dog."*

I held my open palms upward to Heaven and surrendered them in prayer, asking God to guide me and surrendering my will to God's.

I had been talking to a friend who moved to New Zealand the year before with a whole bunch of passionate followers of Jesus with Youth With A Mission (YWAM). She encouraged me during those lean years and saw my hunger for more of God. Like me, she worked in public relations and music and gave it all up to go to the end of the earth in pursuit of a deeper relationship with God. The discipleship school she told me about was in a place called the Bay of Plenty. I was intrigued by the name because I'd been living in a Sea of Poverty for two years—maybe God was trying to transition me into something. School started in July, just two months away. I didn't have money to put gas in the car, and raising money to fly around the world and pay housing expenses was a real leap of imagination.

But I couldn't shake the idea; the more I thought about it, the more excited I became.

WITHIN TWO WEEKS OF PRAYING, God answered my prayer in a painful way. Duncan got ill, barely able to stand on his legs. He would jump up for a walk with the usual perk in his eyes, only to stumble and fall. Other things started happening overnight — his loss of appetite, despondency, and quiet moaning. It was painful for me to see my friend's pain. I begged God to heal him. I took him to veterinarian after veterinarian with no idea how to pay the escalating bills. After a visit to a veterinary oncologist, the doctor reported,

"I don't know what it is, but it's really, really, really bad."

16

CALLED WHERE NO PATH IS LAID

The heron is a majestic bird. It soars with a wingspan unrivaled by most birds. Some herons have blueish scraggly plumage, while others can be pure white. The first time I saw one when I knew it was God speaking to me was on a country drive with my dog. It was an unfamiliar two-lane road in the foothills south of the Adirondacks. I sensed that God was shifting my future and inviting me to go deep with Him, anywhere and everywhere. Duncan was in the car with me because we had another lousy doctor's visit and a colossal bill. I pulled the car to the side of the road and cried. Yellow fields filled with tall grass lined both sides of the road. It was a sunny day, and cars were rushing past. I saw a tall white heron in the field across the street. His neck blended with the golden wheat, and he was close to the road. Sensing God wanted to speak, I grabbed a sheet of paper.

> "I am calling you into the unknown where no path has been laid."

My car swayed from the force of every vehicle that passed. I asked the Lord if I should look for another job after teaching, what I was to do, and how I was to survive. I was overwhelmed and desperate for His direction for my life.

> "Do not take the busy road. Do not get a job, for I am calling you into the unknown."

God told me to look at the thick grass fields and continued,

> "You can't see what's in them, but that is where I call you to. For a while, you will see Me, and then you won't. But I will be there."

The heron tucked into the tall grass and out of my sight. God brought to my mind all the miracles of bills paid and food to eat during the weary months when I couldn't see the shore and only had Jesus as my life preserver. The heron stepped forward from the brush. I sat for a long while mesmerized. The whole time God spoke, the white heron stood motionless at the edge of the tall grass, and Duncan sat quietly on the car's front seat by my side. Shortly, I started the engine and drove toward home with a new measure of trust in my heart, even though I didn't see the resolve for my aching. The pain was still there, but I knew God had heard me and was leading me.

I asked God to take Duncan to rest if healing was not in His plan. Every morning, I awoke and found Duncan curled on the cold tile bathroom floor, stretched against the washing machine's cold metal. I comforted him, sang over him, and petted him. I knew what I had to do, but I wished God had made the decision and not me. He was suffering, and I needed to show compassion toward my furry friend.

Duncan perked up like a puppy when I called him for the final ride in the car. He sniffed the grass for the longest time outside the vet clinic—how I wanted to flee with him in my car and continue to wait for a miracle.

Instead, I led him into the building.

It was Memorial Day weekend, a time to remember. This was God's answer to prayer, but it wasn't easy. Four days later, my friends Ivan and Luis knocked on the door, telling me they wanted to rent my house and make it a men's ministry house. I couldn't answer. Shutting the door, I drove two hours to my parents' lakeside camp. I cried to God.

> *"This is My answer, My daughter. Do you not see? I am leading you into the great adventure you have been asking for."*

The pieces fell into place. Teaching ended, and friends wanted to rent my house. I wondered when the next school year would start in New Zealand and learned it was just two months away, exactly when my job would end.

In my grieving Duncan's passing, I struggled to find hope from God regarding the passing of pets. I couldn't find the Bible clear on whether pets had spirits and could go to Heaven. I was grieving something fierce, and my faith was shaking to wonder at the goodness of God when it came to things like animals we care about. How could a loving God let animals return to the ground with nothing more?

God was merciful to me and gave me not one but two open visions that played like movies before my eyes. The first was a vision of Jesus laughing and spinning in circles as dozens of small furry animals jumped and played around His feet. There were all kinds—rabbits and puppies and kittens and birds and adorable fluffy things. Jesus danced and spun with His hands in the air, and they all pranced and leaped around Him in circles. Among the animals was a small brown puppy. I knew it was Duncan, though I adopted him when he was much bigger. His eyes were locked on Jesus, and he was full of life. The animals were young and joyful, and Jesus played with them.

In the second vision, a ladder descended from Heaven through the roof of my car in a beam of light. The light brought my dog, who sat beside me with his head on my lap. I reached my hands to see if he was real. His thick brown fur scrunched in my fingers as I petted the folds of his neck. The ladder revealed a staircase that led to a hallway of rooms above. It was a warm home, but unfamiliar to me, with worn carpets and yellowed lights. The voice of God called for Duncan to return above the stairs. Duncan climbed the stairs, his body getting younger with every step. Halfway up, he paused and turned back to me. My canine companion locked a fixed, long gaze of sadness mixed with love. Then he turned his head and regally followed the voice of his Creator with an unswerving allegiance to the Most High. The dim yellow lights flickered in the ethereal house made from memories. As suddenly as it began, the light ascended, the car roof appeared, and I was alone. It was a vivid vision that brought healing to my grieving heart.

God doesn't promise that things will be easy, but He walks with us every step of the way and comforts us. Jesus told us there would be sacrifices to be made, and I wondered what was in store for me as I followed after God. I only knew I wanted everything He offered, and I was hungry to learn how much was waiting for me if I followed Him anywhere and entirely depended upon Him.

God made humanity from dirt and air to keep us humble. It is only with His breath that we live. How small and fragile we are, and how beyond our understanding mighty we are in the Spirit with the infilling of Jesus. Only through God's breath and the Spirit's filling can we fully live.

 Everyone who has left houses or brothers or sisters or father or mother or children or property, for My name's sake, will receive a hundred times as much and will inherit eternal life. (Matthew 19:29)

Many are content to live in quaint houses with manicured gardens when a massive oil well lies just below the surface. Are you prepared to uncover your manicured garden to find it?

Get out to the untamed wilderness and into the wild. Get into the meadows and get lost with the Lord. What was so different about Moses, Abraham, David, Peter, and Paul? They were people like you and me. They said *yes* to God and answered the call for the reward of intimacy with God. God leads us today just as He led them years ago.

17

INTO THE DEEP

We are all called deeper with God, every one of us, if we say *yes* and take one faith-filled step at a time. Running after Jesus requires one primary ingredient—Faith. With faith, we listen, we follow, and we trust. Our senses strengthen, and we realize we do hear His voice, whether it is a whisper or a neon sign. Can we let go of everything else and run after Jesus unencumbered?

When I signed up for Jesus, I signed up to have my whole heart burn for Him.

As Jake Hamilton wrote:

> Who's gonna go into God's heart and come back with something so deep and so profound that a generation will be changed?

Things don't make sense in God's Kingdom, but maybe they make more sense than we think. God never forces us to follow; He doesn't demand—*He invites*. God desires that we offer Him the gift of our hearts in surrendered love. How can we not, after everything He has done for us?

C.S. Lewis wrote:

> It would seem that our Lord finds our desires not too strong, but too weak. We are half-hearted creatures, fooling about with drink and sex and ambition when infinite joy is offered us, like an ignorant child who wants to go on making mud pies in a slum because he cannot imagine what is meant by the offer of a holiday at sea. We are far too easily pleased.

The more I fell in love with Jesus, the more of Him I wanted. I was challenged by the words of the rich young man who wanted more of God but couldn't let go of his things; those words of Jesus burned into my thoughts. What would happen if I took Jesus at His Word? The reward of surrender outweighed the rusted sparkle of the world. I was ready for more. I rented my house out and raised a miracle of money to buy an airline ticket to New Zealand. I would spend the next five months learning more profound mysteries in my pursuit of Jesus. We can hold nothing in our hands so we may fully take Jesus' hand in ours.

God calls us to let go.
We are invited to let everything go.

Away from the noise and busyness of this world is a proverbial lake and mountain with a spectacular view. When we press into God's heart, surrendering ourselves fully to the Lord, we see a small wooden boat with two oars resting on that lake. It's as if we are being summoned to a new shore, and our limited understanding of beauty is a fraction of what is waiting when we surrender the skyscrapers from our hands and walk toward the open sea of possibility.

We are sojourners in this world. This world is not our home. The more we remember this, the more we yearn for our true home above. The Temple of God had three chambers to draw worshipers toward God's Holy Presence. We can't stop in the Temple's outer court because all the great stuff is in the inner tent where the Holy of Holies dwells. The mysteries of the Kingdom of God are in the inner tent—the table of bread, the fragrance, the golden lampstand, the sanctuary. When we press into the deep, we surround ourselves with El Shaddai, closely pressed to His heartbeat. We trust Him to lead us into the unknown.

Fear and faith are similar because both believe something that hasn't yet happened will happen. Fear makes you concerned about yourself. Faith focuses on what God is going to do. Fear tries to strike at the heart of God's people to keep them from taking a step of faith. Faith steps off the branch and trusts its wings to fly.

Are you brave enough to go deeper where the water is over your head? You can stay splashing and wading in the pool's shallow end, where it's safe. You'll still get wet. But you'll get to Heaven in a baby stroller instead of a chariot. Do you want to enter Heaven as a baby newly born or a mature son of God who knows his Father's business? You may be in the same waters in the same pool—but not everyone will have the same experience amidst that water. That part is up to you.

Jesus made the disciples get into the boat and go ahead of Him to the other side of the lake while He dismissed the crowd. Then He went up on a mountainside by Himself to pray. When we detach from the crowd, God's training begins. We start to look more like Jesus and less like the world. The world may think we're weird, but we believe just the same: a world full of people who don't walk in the power of God is weird.

We weren't meant to fit in. We were born to stand out.

I PACKED up the houseful of possessions and stored them in the basement. I rented the house to my friends for the next year and flew from New York to New Zealand. God provided every dollar. My faith soared. After two grueling years of falling into bed each night exhausted and covered with either paint or baby barf from nannying, I looked forward to six months in the Bay of Plenty, a far cry away from the tunnel of poverty. I would sit at the Lord's feet and drink from His proverbial cup. My only responsibility would be feeding baby cows on our farm, a chore I looked forward to daily. There was a cafeteria for all our meals, and there was no more collecting food at food pantries and filling my kitchen with sauces and bread. It was time to be filled up in a honeymoon season with Jesus and all my needs met. I would soak in teaching from other missionaries who walked the walk and taught from life experience rather than books. Our only book was the Bible, and we had worship every day.

There was a chapel for us to go to and have quiet time in, and there were several one-room huts anyone could use to get alone with God. I preferred to walk the cow pastures in my quiet time to talk to God. There was a rise in the land where I could get away from everyone and be with trees and sky, the cows and sheep. I prayed and processed everything we were learning, with full days in the classroom and worship five days a week.

An African missionary encouraged me not to view discipleship training as interrupting life.

 "The higher the edifice, the deeper the foundation. If you think your foundation is already deep," she said, "make it deeper."

She told me about a newlywed couple who joined her team in Africa. Although their zeal was evident, their foundation in the Lord wasn't strong. Within a year, their marriage ended in divorce from adultery. As solid as I thought my faith was, I didn't understand the healing I needed, like peels of an onion. We never stop growing; we never stop strengthening our spirits. I initially felt awkward when I realized many students were half my age. They helped me overcome my hurdles through their unjaded vigor for life. God knows what we need. The tallest buildings need to have the deepest foundations, and there's no such thing as too much time invested with God.

At one point during the discipleship training, I felt like I was going backward. I took long walks in the fields and felt like my insides were ripping apart. I didn't know who I was any longer. I knew God was doing something in me, but it hurt. That's when God showed me. He gave me a picture of a road needing to be repaved. Growing up in upstate New York with harsh winters, I knew how bad the roads got from expansion and contraction due to temperatures. Most years, the maintenance crew would fill potholes with tar as a short-term economic fix, but the road was bumpy. The only way to fix the roads when they got torn up was to rip out the pavement, break it apart, pour new gravel, and lay new pavement. The result was a smooth, glassy road that was delightful to drive on. God showed me He was tearing up my foundation because He wanted to repave it completely. It got messy before it got better. But I had a beautiful, solid foundation, and my potholes were fully repaired.

> *"Come up, come away. Get out of the current of the world. I want to teach you to fly."*

Recognizing the voice of God is the right of every one of His children. It can be a nudge in the heart to contact someone or do something. It can be a word dropped in the spirit after a prayer. If you know God, then you know His voice. It's like picking up the phone and hearing your best friend's voice.

In Ephesians 1:17-18 Paul writes:

 I keep asking that the God of our Lord Jesus Christ may give you the Spirit of wisdom and revelation, so that you may know him better. I pray that the eyes of your heart may be enlightened so that you may know the hope to which he has called you, the riches of his glorious inheritance.

One day, I drove by a hitchhiking woman. As I drove past her, the Holy Spirit quickened to me to return and get her. I didn't want to because I wanted a quiet drive with the Lord. He reminded me that while this was our journey together, I could trust Him and let Him unravel my plans. Reluctantly, I turned the car and circled back, half hoping she was gone. But she was still there. As she got in the car, she told me she had been praying and asking God to send somebody to help her. Her husband was away, and they only had one car. I told her the Lord told me to help her. We talked about the Lord for the thirty-minute drive. When I dropped her off, she put a hundred-dollar bill in my hand, telling me God told her to give it to me. She did not know I needed exactly that amount—I secretly prayed that need to the Lord.

ONE TIME, as part of our discipleship training, we divided our school of forty students into teams of eight or nine people, and each team drove to different parts of the nation for a three-day faith journey. We were to seek the Kingdom of God first. We were told to trust God to care for our needs as He promised.

Our nine men and women were allowed to bring just a backpack with water, a toothbrush, a Bible, and a change of clothes: no cell phones, no food, and no money. We had a full tank of gas and twenty dollars only to be used in an emergency. Our mission was to offer help to anyone we could and not mention or think of our personal needs. We were to trust God to provide shelter and food. We drove two hours to a small surfing village called Raglan. It was a cold rainy day, and we were already hungry, but we parked the van and approached various shops, asking if anyone needed help. We sorted clothes at a thrift shop and carried parcels for a gardener. One woman offered us shelter from the rain and hot tea and biscuits, for which we were thankful. We approached a Maori medical clinic to provide our help for a few days. The woman behind the desk looked at us strangely and asked if we had a place to stay.

"No," we replied. The rain was pouring down.

"Come back at five o'clock if you don't have a place to stay," she said.

We drove back to town, helped where possible, and then returned to the clinic. The woman led us to her home and pointed to a pile of mats to sleep on in an aluminum garage. We tried not to grumble. She fed us some awful soup of things thrown carelessly in a pot. It was hot, and we ate it in gulps. The rain pelted on the metal roof. The following day, the nine of us worked hard helping her on her property, filling barrels with weeds from wet gardens and shucking buckets of oysters collected from the ocean. She told us she was the Maori chief wife and this was the local base. She told us she was nervous when we came to her because she heard God tell her to invite us back, but she didn't want to. It turns out they were all Christians.

Later that evening, she announced that she and the chief were preparing a banquet for us. They cooked all the hundreds of oysters we shucked that day and unique dishes from their farm that were so delicious. With full bellies, we passed around a guitar and sang worship songs. They taught us Maori songs. We taught them English songs. That night, she invited the girls in our group to stay inside. On the third day, after working and sharing life with her family and tribe members, no one wanted us to leave. We hugged and took photos, and none of us would ever forget those three days.

 Do not worry about what you will eat or what you will drink or what you will wear. The pagans eagerly pursue all these things, yet your Father in Heaven knows that you need all these. But seek first the Kingdom of God and His righteousness, and all these things shall be added to you. (Matthew 6:31-33)

So many faith adventures during that season would be the foundation for years. Jesus tells His followers to cast out demons. I had done a fair share of that in New York, but it was usually with some fear and trepidation. I was getting God's heart of compassion to see people suffering and want to help them break the bonds of their oppressors. Jesus is that bond-breaker; we carry His excellent news everywhere we go. Once, we had a team serving at youth camps in the South Island and reaching out to teenagers in after-school programs with the good news about Jesus. We held plays, taught songs, gave testimonies, hung out with kids, and listened to their problems.

At a church youth retreat, there was a fourteen-year-old girl in a crowd of hundreds whom I saw a bright light over. God was highlighting her to me. The speaker called our team to the front to pray for any teen who wanted to come up. I knew that girl would come to me, and God wanted me to pray for her. She stood up from her seat and walked straight up to me. I smiled and asked if she had Jesus in her heart. She said no. I asked if she wanted to invite Jesus into her heart. She said yes. As easy as that, I led her in a prayer of salvation. Seeing how God shined His light and ushered the runway for her soul to belong to Jesus was beautiful. Her eternal destiny was changed in a moment.

Another girl, sixteen, was in a crowd at a teen worship night. Everyone was praising God with hands held high. This girl's body shook as if the power of God was jolting her. But I knew in the Spirit of the Lord that it was not God's power that was shaking her but the enemy's. I saw the Spirit of death shaking her. God directed me to stand beside her during the loud worship. I quietly placed my hand on her shoulder and commanded the Spirit of death to leave her at once in Jesus' name. The girl convulsed as soon as I prayed that, and the evil spirit left her. Anyone watching would have thought I put my hand on her; I didn't want to embarrass but help her. When worship ended, she ran up to me, bursting with excitement. She told me that she had secretly been making plans to take her life for thirty days. She was obsessed with the idea. Not even her closest friends knew. God set her free from that tormenting spirit.

Sometimes, God asks us to do things we might feel awkward about, and we don't know what's on the other side of that obedience. In this case, it was the girl's life. We don't always find out the impact on this side of Heaven. Being a modern-day water walker is simply obeying one step at a time. We run with Jesus and take captive every fear-of-man thought. We can't be bothered if we look silly in the world's eyes.

The water ripples out and never stops bubbling and bringing life.

18

BE HOLY AS I AM HOLY

To walk with Jesus is to become more like Him every day. The blood of Jesus redeems us in the waters of baptism. But that is the beginning of sanctification, cleaning up the fish. We are called to be holy.

Be holy in all you do, just as God, who called you, is holy. It is written in First Peter 1:15-16:

 You must be holy because I am holy.

David was called a man after God's heart. David trusted God and worshiped Him freely. He built his palace in the lowest part of the Kidron Valley because the place where God would dwell would be at the highest point. Unlike kings who built their palaces on top of mountains to look down on their kingdom and have the advantage of seeing enemies advance from a distance, David declared his help came from God. David petitioned God to examine his heart and humbled himself before God, praying in Psalm 139:

Search me, O God, and know me. Examine me, know my anxious thoughts, see if there is any offensive way within me, and lead me in the everlasting way.

David revered the Presence of God that resided in the ark of the covenant as he transported it from Israel's wilderness to its final home in Jerusalem. The last time David tried to move the ark and it started tipping over, God struck dead the men who tried to steady the cart with their hands. David feared God and wanted to please the Lord. He sacrificed a bull and a fattened calf every six paces out of reverence. *Can you imagine every six steps, making a sacrifice unto the Lord?*

Another attribute of David was that he was a man who earnestly asked the Lord to search his heart and remove any wicked thing. David spent years in the desert fleeing Saul, and he knew homelessness and hunger. He knew fear and faith. He delighted in the Lord and relied upon God. David built his palace in the valley so that God's dwelling place in the Temple would be what he would look up towards, praying in Psalm 121:

 I lift my eyes to the mountains. Where does my help come from? My help comes from the Lord, the Maker of Heaven and Earth.

In First Samuel 13, God boasted that David was "a man after God's heart." It wasn't because of perfection, for David made some big mistakes. We are called to be holy by seeking God daily to search and refine us to be more like Jesus. We desire to please God and remove sin from our lives to walk in holiness with our Father.

We walk more and more in purity and holiness daily when we invite God to help us. Ask God to forgive you so you can be pleasing in His sight so that He will not take His Presence away from you. Jesus summed up the Law in two commandments in Matthew 22:

 You shall love the Lord you God with all your heart, and with all your soul, and with all your mind. This is the first and greatest commandment. The second is that you shall love your neighbor as yourself.

Jesus took it up a notch when He said that if we even consider a sinful thought, it is as if we committed that sin. Everything in Scripture is summarized in those two commandments because if we truly love our neighbor, we wouldn't covet their things or curse them. If we truly love our God, we would not have idols in our hearts nor anything against His will for us. Our hearts would be postured like David's with the daily plea to be clean and acceptable before our holy God.

Satan is the accuser of the saints of God, telling God how rotten His kids are while telling us that God can't be trusted. He is a cruel master from whom we must run. He will use any Achilles' heel to afflict people. It could be a trauma or abuse; it could be a sin or thought or action, or it could be through the bloodline of your ancestors. We need Jesus, the only One who can redeem us from the bondage of sin and death. Who the Son set free is free indeed. We run into God's outstretched arms.

When we repent of a sin, it is forgotten by God and covered by Jesus' blood. You can testify boldly when Satan tries to bring you before God's throne of judgment.

"Yes, it's true, I did those sins. But it is under the blood of Jesus now."

Jesus is our defender from the accuser of the brethren. We have the assurance in Hebrews 4 that we have a great High Priest who has passed through the heavens, Jesus, the Son of

God. We come boldly to God's throne of grace, holding fast to our confession to obtain mercy and grace.

The powers of Hell sniff like wolves looking for doorways to enter and afflict their victims. Fear is a big door. A foggy memory haunted me since I was five, playing like a movie in my head. I sat alone in the car while my mom ran into the bank. Another vehicle parked next to ours with four hideous women. They stared at me with evil transfixed in their eyes. I couldn't scream. A dark presence paralyzed me. I felt hands around my neck.

Finally, my mother returned, and we drove off. I never discussed it. The spirit of fear attached to me that afternoon. I panicked anytime we passed that bank. After that, I would be pinned to the bedroom carpet by a force of evil.

I became accident-prone and would get stitches or casts every year. A sledding accident. Falling downstairs. Slipping in a mud puddle and breaking my arm. Clammy skin and fainting spells. Breaking my foot at the public library. Crazy stories that happened often enough to pause and wonder if another force was operating. My parents got tired of taking me to the hospital, which made me feel worse. Evil pushed me beyond reason. Hell was bent on killing me. Ephesians 6 warns us not to wrestle against flesh and blood but against evil principalities and powers.

Jesus teaches us how to take authority in His name. Years later, I had a bad case of the flu, and when I commanded the spirit of illness to leave me in Jesus' name, I saw a dark shadowy spirit cower at the end of my bed and then flee as if it were being whipped. It was a wild thing to see, and I realized how real the spirit world is and the authority of Jesus over every power and principality.

How do we discover and deal with these open doors? We must be born again through the blood of Jesus, to whom every spirit bows. Through repentance, we stand on the power of

Jesus' propitiation and clean our house one door and room at a time. We fortify our home so those wolves cannot find entry, sealing everything with the saving blood of Jesus.

I visited a girl with piles of Twilight movies, Anime, horror movies, and spirit dreamcatchers. The evil spirits tried to suffocate me when I entered her house. I was in the enemy's camp, and he had a legal invitation to be there; my arrival stirred up a war between Heaven and Hell. I warned her of the doors she had opened that permitted evil to torment her. She wasn't interested, and all I could do was let my peace return to me as I left. We can't force someone's freedom, but it is a beautiful gift from God when we submit to His Lordship for our lives.

Below is a non-exhaustive list as you pray through areas and seek forgiveness from the Lord. If you feel a quickening in your spirit at something in this list, ask God to bring it to light. The Holy Spirit will guide you. Repent by asking forgiveness from God, then receive God's forgiveness. After receiving forgiveness, command any evil spirits to leave in Jesus' name. They won't have legal permission to stay. Let the peace of God fill you.

Freedom is a beautiful gift from God. Breathe in the fresh air and live in that freedom.

- Any gods or idols besides Adonai, the God of Abraham, Isaac, and Jacob
- Adding or subtracting from God's word
- New Age, occult, witchcraft, magic
- Mind control, hypnosis
- Communicating with the dead
- Fantasy, horoscope, tarot, palmistry
- Blood pacts, oaths, covenants
- Freemasonry, secret societies
- Horror/fear-related films/books

- Harry Potter, Pokemon, Anime, Dungeons and Dragons
- Amulets, charms, fetishes, crystals
- Yoga, Acupuncture
- Cults
- Satanism, sacrifices
- Abortion (both male and female involvement)
- Hatred
- Unforgiveness (to others, to oneself, to God)
- Bitterness
- Rebellion
- Lying
- Self-mutilation
- Sexual sins, lust, adultery, fornication, homosexuality, perversion
- Trauma, frequent accidents
- Satanic ritual abuse
- Incest
- Worship/idolatry of a person, team, self
- Jealousy
- Greed
- Substance abuse, smoking, drunkenness
- Addictions
- Anger, rage, violence, murder, control
- Stealing
- Slander, gossip, meddling
- Crude joking, coarse language
- Pride, narcissism
- Shame, unworthiness
- Gluttony
- Vanity, haughtiness
- Blaspheming God
- Putting your will above God's (statements such as I will, I won't)

Be Holy as I Am Holy

THERE ARE MORE extensive deliverance resources available. This is a condensed list to help you get started. Pray through and take time to seek the Lord. If you were the victim or perpetrator, in thought or action, ask God to help you forgive and repent. If someone comes to mind who you do not desire to bless and wish joy and peace, this indicates that you may still have some healing and forgiveness to work through. Remember, the Lord commands us to forgive. When we do, He can start the healing process in you. We are simply releasing our judgment and asking God for mercy. Imagining anyone in the agony of Hell for eternity is an awful thought. We have been forgiven much. Shouldn't we extend mercy and forgiveness? It isn't always easy, but it is critical. As we measure and judge, so are we measured and judged by God.

Love covers a multitude of sins. We are not called to be victims but overcomers. We can abandon unhealthy situations while shaking the dust from our feet. But remember—the enemy is not fleshly but spiritual. Do not fuel his fire with anger and hatred. We belong to God through Christ, so we must demonstrate His nature, even as He said from the cross,

 "Father, forgive them, for they know not what they do."

SHEEP STORY

For a few months, I lived in a cottage in New Zealand and tended a paddock of sheep. One afternoon, I was weeding the garden beds and threw the weeds over the fence for them to eat. Six fluffy fat sheep watched, and one began to nibble. Among the weeds was green ivy with sticky leaves. I thought the sheep would eat it and didn't know it was a nuisance. In it went. The ivy stuck to the sheep's wool. The more the sheep nibbled, the more the ivy tangled around it. The sheep was agitated and dragged its head on the grass. It got stuck worse. The sheep panicked, so I climbed over the rail to help. The sheep took one look at me and bolted.

I crouched low, trying to approach slowly. The animal's front, face, and eyes was drowning in green ivy. It bleated loudly and dodged my attempt to help. I found a long stick and tried to get close enough to brush the ivy. The sheep ran. Unable to help, I left the paddock.

I could have spared the sheep the distress it was suffering. It dragged its head and shook its coat while the other sheep looked on disinterestedly. I thought this is how God must feel when we have something stuck on us. We run away or don't think it's a big deal. We wear ourselves out. We bleat. We panic. We have green stuck all over our faces. God waits, throws His hands up, saying wearily,

"My child, won't you let Me help you?"

You can't keep dragging your head in the dirt forever. Just let Him help you. He's a very good parent.

> It is for freedom that Christ has set us free. Stand firm, then, and do not let yourselves be burdened again by a yoke of slavery. (Galatians 5:1)

19

THIS IS WAR

Early in my walk with the Lord, I was zealous to take down every principality in my passion for God. I was on dangerous ground because the Lord did not call me to do that. The Bible says the battle belongs to the Lord. He is always victorious, but we need to know when He calls us to battle and when we are not to engage. We must walk closely with God to discern His voice. We may not escape without injuries if we go to the battle frontlines of our willful volition.

Before heading to New Zealand, I was back in New York, and a friend asked for help. He was renting an apartment in an old Shaker mansion and grumbled that there was paranormal activity in the house. He asked a group of us to anoint his apartment with oil, so we agreed. I didn't have a clear word from the Lord to go, and I would not have consented to go if I knew how infested with demons his property was.

We entered a wormhole at the front door like a spiritual water tunnel. We were in a translucent bubble of rippling fog as we climbed the enormous staircase of the old mansion with apartments at every door. A paranormal squad measured paranormal seismology on the landing of the stairs. I realized God did not direct me there, but I didn't want to let my friend down. We entered his apartment. I told him to anoint his walls and assert his domain in Jesus' name. I told him his Chinese dragon art had to go, but he didn't want to throw them. I probably should have left at that point, but I sat on the floor instead, removing my guitar from its case.

I took a breath, but two hands squeezed around my throat. I couldn't breathe. I squeaked out the beginning of the song, *How Great Is Our God*, and the hands loosened from my neck. As we sang, I heard blood-curdling screams outside the window like witches boiling in oil.

I sang four worship songs and then quickly bolted, urging our friend to move, you're on your own if you stay, good luck, etc. We were leaving, and it felt like we were fleeing for our lives. You might say you were nice, you helped a friend.

Our hearts were in the right place, but we did not have a word from the Lord to do that assignment.

Friends, we were in a spiritual war zone. We must clearly hear and then do what God instructs. We cannot put God to the test by stepping out with zeal but not wisdom. We need God's leading. When Jesus' disciples were beaten up by demons, Jesus explained they didn't go about it the right way.

> Victory comes when zeal is meted with Godly counsel and a clear word from the Lord.

Shortly after, one of the friends who participated that day developed an undiagnosable skin affliction where the skin fell off her body, and she was covered in sores. She suffered years of prayer and doctors before she finally got well.

I had battle wounds, too. Within a month, I was rushed three times by ambulance to the hospital with severe chest pains. It felt like broken glass in my windpipe, and I could feel someone's hands squeezing. I stayed nine nights in the hospital. X-rays showed a mysterious puncture hole in my left lung like a popped balloon. For a year, I wore sterile gloves and masks and was on a constant course of liquid oxygen and steroids. I did nebulizer treatments every two hours on a massive machine from the hospital. My immune system plummeted, and no doctor understood why. I prayed and cried to the Lord for healing. I learned I had legal claim to every square inch I owned to bind unclean spirits, but I went into someone else's domain, where God didn't call. Until I had God's revelation of the legal rights the enemy had to afflict me, I could not shake it free.

God is indeed bigger. God can handle it. But like in a war, when a submarine pops its telescopic lens above water only to find it dead-center in the middle of a ring of submarine war bombers, all aimed and ready, you put God in a tough place. God doesn't want us to test Him, which is why Jesus would not fling Himself from the top of the Holy Temple when Satan tempted Him. Our little worship posse inadvertently popped our periscope into a portal of Hell when we visited that apartment, and the aftermath from the onslaught took years to overcome.

It was not until several years later. I was ministering in New Zealand and had a friend airmail me monthly medicines. I had to go to the hospital overseas repeatedly for nebulizer treatments. But I refused to let that keep me from ministering to the Lord. I trusted Him for my eventual healing. I completed the missionary discipleship program on the North Island, where God healed the deepest places of my heart, and those patched potholes were thoroughly repaired.

OUR SCHOOL SPENT four hours every Thursday in a worship and prayer room where God downloaded visions like moving pictures in my spirit. I had a treasury of prophetic words directly from the Father, and I was thankful for the season to go deeper with the Lord.

One encounter with God in the prayer room left me unable to speak for a day; I had to write notes if I needed to say something. It was crazy; I'd never been impacted to that level by God before.

God poured into me with an overflowing love.

IN THE SEVENTH month in New Zealand, God brought prophetic revelation through another pastor for my healing. I was hiking up a small mountain to pray with a group of pastors, and I had to stop often to use an inhaler. He asked how long I had been dealing with this problem.

"About three years."

He asked if there was something I was doing when it started, and I recalled the apartment nightmare. He told me he saw a spiritual witchcraft dagger in my left lung. I was astounded. I never told anyone about the mysterious hole in my left lung.

"That dagger is still there. Do you want us to remove it?"

So, on top of that mountain, they all prayed. My chest got tight, and something tried to throw my body to the ground. Finally, it left with spastic coughs. They prayed against geographic spirits and witchcraft spirits that had attacked me. I was finally free.

When I walk into homes, I ask the Lord what's happening there and whether He wants me to do something. A year after the prayer on the mountain, I was completely free of medications and received an excellent health bill from my doctor. I shared my testimony with my other afflicted friend, which helped her begin her turnaround. Praise God for revelation and discerning believers.

Some lessons we learn the hard way from an overzealous spirit wanting to take possession of all the land. God warned the Israelites that they could not take it at once when they entered the Promised Land, lest wild beasts attack. Things must be done in God's time and in God's way. The lesson in all of this was that it was not our battle.

We have authority in Jesus, but only as He leads. Otherwise, we're just kids hitting a giant piñata and have no idea what will fall out. As we learn to take authority, God will give us more territory. The battle is the Lord's; we submit our wills for Him to lead us. May His will be done.

South Island Snake

We talked a lot about deliverance and spiritual warfare at school. I had had my fair share of deliverance and warfare. But what I had seen so far would be small compared to the principalities God would reveal. I had to abide under God's protective wing more than ever. Jesus said He would only do what He saw His Father do. Walking hand in hand closely with Father God would be my means of survival.

After school ended, I moved to New Zealand's majestic South Island to process everything. I and another student lived with a Christian family. I quickly discerned something wasn't right. The tension in the house grew, and the airwaves for me to speak with God became scrambled with static. It was a spiritual heaviness. No matter how many hours I paced the backyard trying to pray, it was as if my words hit a shield and bounced back to the ground. Confusion manifested. I started doubting everything I knew about my Father.

I prayed in tongues for hours, trying to hear the voice of my Daddy. There was a thick, black, impenetrable shroud. I could only feel His presence when I drove off the property a few miles down the road. Something was interfering. I found out what it was. There was unconfessed sin and unforgiveness. The woman admitted things to me but refused to repent. She was angry and bitter. She undermined her husband and was a rogue self-proclaimed prophet the area churches shunned. I was shocked when she boasted she would never forgive them.

On top of that, the house sat on property once belonging to a Masonic lodge. I felt in the Spirit like my friend and I were in a python grip. One night, I drove a few miles in the car someone loaned me so I could talk to God. I felt like I was kickboxing shadows in the dark, and I asked God to expose my adversary to me. I prayed.

> *"Only if it is Your will, Lord, pull back the veil and let me see what I am against."*

He answered my prayer that night. I woke with an alarming vision. There was an enormous white snake over the conservatory next to my bedroom, its coils over the house and yard. A sheet of plexiglass sat above the property, and I saw from below the snake's enormous coils as if looking up through the bottom of an aquarium. The snake was outside my room and in a striking position. Its head crouched and its tongue darted. It hissed two words in a long, drawn-out slither.

"Get... out!"

I ran like Elijah when he ran and hid from Jezebel. Two weeks later, I returned to the house after hiding in Queenstown with friends. The snake was circling my friend, guarding him as prey with its bald head and slanted eyes. My friend was wound up in the coils. All I could do was pray.

I spoke with another prophet in the area. She agreed the household was up against a spirit.

This is War

"Do you know which spirit you are dealing with?" she asked.

I whispered, "Yes. Jezebel."

I have heard of it before but never encountered the principality face-to-face. One month earlier, I volunteered to help in the kitchen at a nearby Christian center, where my friend discerned that spirit operating through this woman. When she commanded the spirit to leave the camp, the woman fled hysterically, disappearing for the entire week of camp, leaving me to figure out how to cook six meals a day for a hundred and twenty teenagers. Jezebel, operating in conjunction with Leviathan and the spirits of confusion, witchcraft, rebellion, emasculation, rage, and murder, needed to be bound daily from me and my friend. God gave me authority over it in Jesus' name, so I bound its witchcraft, confusion, curses, and interference, persistently praying Ephesians four and bathing my mind under God's truth. Unbelief, confusion, and bitterness tried to muddle my thoughts. This was no longer boot camp. God was training me for war. When the Lord permitted me to leave the house, He spoke to me.

"I will bring Jezebel down. I will destroy that seven-fold demon spirit."

We learn to hear God's voice and follow His leading. We must sharpen our ears to have spiritual discernment so we can partner with God to defeat the enemy and his pit of vipers. I learned the life-saving importance of hiding under God's wing like a chick with its mother. I had to lean into God's strength, not my own.

As I grew with the Lord, my zeal for God became tempered in wisdom and maturity. I was learning not to swing my piñata stick blindfolded to poke blindly at the demonic realm like a hornet's nest. I would minister unto the Lord later in Jerusalem, the spiritual epicenter of the world. The lessons in warfare from the South Island would save my life in the land where bigger Spiritual giants roamed.

Ants on An Elephant

One of God's most challenging lessons is to lighten up. We can take ourselves too seriously. God is battling; we get to go along for the ride. I once heard a story that helped put things in perspective and remind me to stay humble before the Lord.

It's a story of an elephant crossing a rope bridge over a deep river far below. A bunch of ants were on the back of the elephant. The bridge shook with every step. It swayed left, then right, left, then right. The ants looked nervously down at the raging rapids below. They held on tight while the elephant crossed. They worried the bridge might break. When the elephant finally reached the other side, the ants jumped up and down on its back, shouting with glee.

"Yay! Hooray! We shook the bridge! We shook the bridge!"

I smile and think often of that story when I think it's me and not God doing the bridge shaking. Like a parent baking cookies with their toddler, we all know it would be a whole lot quicker and easier if the parent did it by themselves. The kitchen wouldn't be a mess of flour and eggs and sticky fingers. But God delights in co-laboring with us—it is important to Him that we know and learn from our heavenly parent. He wants us to grow in wisdom and maturity through Him.

> But let's remember who is shaking the bridge
> and give *Him* all the glory.

We are indeed interfacing with heavy spiritual forces in a world emaciated without knowing Jesus, but we shouldn't have serious faces. The *joy* of the Lord is our strength. His happiness is over us, and He has equipped us to succeed and not fail.

When we worship, we are warring in the Spirit. When we feast at the Lord's banqueting table, our enemy looks on, unable to touch us. When we are close to the Lord's side, we are safe. We are like cubs nestled under the protection of the Lion of Judah.

One evening, Jesus woke me repeatedly as I tried to sleep. I had been wrestling with anxious thoughts, tossing and turning. The world's cares were weighing on me, and I was overwhelmed.

"Lighten up, and let the cards fall where they may."

What an unusual thing for God to speak. He told me to chill out, and I saw His eyes pierce through me with a steady love that burned away worry. Before my eyes, He changed into a mighty lion and looked at me a long time with a powerful gaze. He stood very still. Then, as if a movie were playing before my eyes, I saw a dark, bottomless canyon; I was on the cliff's ledge looking down.

Lights flashed around me in a spinning whirl, and time and space collapsed into a black hole that held the universe all wrinkled together in a funnel of rotating lights. Nothing and everything swirled together. I fell into the spinning funnel and let go of fear and worry. It was wonderful and strange toppling into the vortex of light spinning around me, as the lion's eyes told me, without words, I would always be safe with Him, even if nothing seemed certain.

In *The Great Divorce*, C.S. Lewis paints a picture of Heaven, describing all the filth of Hell contained in a minuscule soil speck in Heaven. He describes Heaven's colors as so supernaturally vivid that the palette on Earth seems like monotone grays and whites in comparison. It's a unique perspective on God's unlimited creativity. Our ability to see what we do not yet know is thinly veiled. We are seated with Christ in the heavens, not just in the age to come but presently. From this perspective, we see clearly.

We flow in power and love from that perspective because we have the viewpoint from the throne of God.

20

STORMS AND AUTHORITY

> The boat was a long way from land, tossed around by the waves, for the wind was against it.
> (Matthew 14:24)

Have you ever been at sea in a storm? As an exchange student at university, I traveled around Europe with friends. We parted for a week, so I went alone to Ireland, putting an 'X' on a street corner on a map of Paris, where we planned to meet the following Tuesday at three in the afternoon. Nervous excitement swept over me when their train departed, and I was alone. I traveled solo across the city to the ferry harbor. Boarding the ferry, I searched for a place to sleep for the twenty-hour sail. I went to the outer deck and claimed the floor between two rows of metal benches. I watched the sea roll all night and bang the swinging door. The rudders rumbled. The temperature dropped, and the wind roared as the night drew on. The wind shifted the vessel, and sleeping bodies rolled on the deck floor with each wave swell. I had never sailed on open seas. I tied my sheet corners to the bolted chairs and wrapped myself like a burrito so I wouldn't fly across the floor. At last, many hours later, the emerald cliffs of Ireland welcomed us to Rosslaer Harbor.

Imagine how scared the twelve disciples of Jesus were on the Sea of Galilee when the storm kicked up. For many of them, the sea was their livelihood, and they had fished upon it for years. It must have been a storm like never before to make them so petrified as their boat tossed. Local Galileans claim such violent storms can manifest and frighten even the most experienced sailor.

The disciples set off in the small wooden fishing boat in familiar waters. They did not expect this life-threatening storm. Jesus showed them a different mode of operation—that of Heaven and not Earth. The disciples would have to trust Jesus and learn to walk in the Spirit, not the flesh. Jesus was about to teach them to walk supernaturally. He would demonstrate how even the wind and seas obey Him.

There is a difference between power and authority. One example that demonstrates this is a diesel truck and a police officer. A diesel truck has power. But the police officer has authority. A person vested in authority, no matter how small in size, can make the truck stop. This is who we are when we are under Christ's authority. We become co-heirs. Jesus has all authority in Heaven and Earth. This means we partake in the rewards and God-given heritage of Jesus—only through Jesus.

We are assured of victory through Jesus, promised in the book of Isaiah in chapter 54, verse 17:

 No weapon formed against you shall prosper, and you shall condemn every tongue that rises against you in judgment. This is the inheritance of the servants of the Most High God, and this is their vindication from Me.

Nothing can stand up to the power and authority of the Almighty God through His Son Jesus. Everything submits to this name.

My friend Graham shared a vision he had in which Jesus took him into Hell. The floor went down slowly as if he and Jesus were in a tall elevator; when the doors opened, Graham was standing with Jesus in Hell. Jesus walked slowly and confidently. My friend stayed very close to Jesus' side, seeing demons everywhere. As they walked, a massive sea of demons scrambled to make way for them to pass. The bigger demons hurried to hide behind smaller ones. They were large and grotesque and very strange looking. They walked toward a throne where Satan was seated. Jesus reached the throne, held out His hand without saying a word, and Satan handed over the keys. They were no longer his because he was defeated when Jesus became the perfect lamb of God when He gave up His life on the cross to overcome the powers of sin, Hell, and death. So, with the keys in His hand, Jesus walked calmly back to the elevator shaft with Graham at His side while demons desperately scrambled to get out of the way. They know who Jesus is, and they shudder at His name.

When we walk with Jesus, we need to know who He is and the power and authority He emanates. We go wherever He calls us because Jesus is Victor.

Every victory belongs to Jesus.

When Jesus slept in the boat during a storm, He was leading them to the center of the storm to show them how to overcome it. When they woke Him, He rose and rebuked the storm, and it was subdued. Storms are not for avoiding but overcoming. We can only cross through or over them with our hand in Jesus' hand, and our eyes locked on Him to lead us.

WE ARE one body through Jesus. Jesus is the head of the body. We are to have the singular mind of Christ and be submitted to His Lordship. When the disciples were tossed on the stormy sea, they were frightened when they saw Jesus walking on the water ahead of them. He was leading the way. Jesus walked ahead on the waves, the same waves that threatened to sink the small boat. Jesus demonstrated a different way, how all of creation submits to His Lordship.

Nothing is impossible when the body stays tethered to the head, Jesus. A bird's wings cannot be stretched inside a nest; wind and gravity will awaken its wings and draw out the instinct to fly. Our nature is not yet fully realized; only through Jesus can we tap into the potential of what slumbers inside the seed from Heaven we contain.

We live through Christ, dead to ourselves, to fulfill our destined purpose. Each of us began as a scroll in Heaven. We carry a dream of God within us. Our reason for existence is tied to this dream from God's heart. The enemy resists it, trying to disqualify us and building a case against us that is settled in the court of Heaven. Our defense is Jesus. We have an accuser of the brethren, Satan, and a mighty defender—Jesus.

God calls us to fulfill our destiny. We are justified by Jesus to be declared innocent by confession of sin. Everything with a Kingdom purpose has a book defining its reason for existence. What are your days destined to be? Before Time, God already knew every opposition you would face and had already prepared a success strategy for you to be an overcomer. Only through Jesus can we walk in glorious victory—because He lives in us. This is why it is critical to repent for everything, big or small, and keep a clean account with God as the judge.

We do not want to allow any loopholes for Satan to accuse us. He has legal permission in God's court to use our words and actions against us, even things we said in frustration. Remove Satan's legal rights so God can answer your prayers. Stand under the powerful witness of Jesus' blood that testifies in your defense. The verdict is sealed but neds execution and enforcement. The Bible tells us, in Colossians 2, that Jesus wiped out the legal documents that had been formed against us, nailing them to the cross and disarming principalities and power. The devil cannot resist this because Jesus' sacrifice was perfect. The blood was the legal transaction.

We can succeed in fulfilling our books based on this truth rather than on our merit. We walk boldly in this truth and are humble because God's lovingkindness showed us undeserved grace. Our response is faith, love, and trust.

We keep our eyes on Jesus, our defender in the court of God. We know we can do nothing apart from Him. Where He calls us, we follow. When Jesus' disciples were in the boat on the stormy water, Peter saw Jesus walking toward the other side, where He told them He would meet them. Jesus was walking on the waves—the same waves that tossed the boat around. Seeing on the water, Peter felt an urgency to be with Him. He called out to Jesus, asking Jesus to invite him to walk on the water.

Jesus said, "Come."

Peter took his first step on the raging sea. His feet did not sink. He was experiencing the exhilaration of walking with Jesus and the authority Jesus has over everything. It was only when Peter looked down at the waves that he started to sink. We can walk upon every storm when our eyes are fixed on Jesus.

Walking closely with Jesus empowers us, through His authority, to defy nature's limitations because Jesus is sovereign over everything.

21

SCHOOL OF THE HOLY SPIRIT

How can you hear God's voice? What does it mean to hear God like Samuel did as a boy? We test everything we sense in the Spirit by God's Word. God wants His children to listen to His voice and respond. The goal is relationship, not religion. Relationship requires friendship and intimacy—open, two-way communication. We feel God's extravagant peace when He moves; we sense His presence and move accordingly. God leads us as He has led the Israelites in the desert with a pillar of smoke. God can speak to us as He did to Moses through a burning bush. He can show His glory as He did on the mountainside in the gentle breeze for Elijah.

God is not limited in how He communicates if we sensitize ourselves to listen. While learning about God is essential through His past miracles, as children of God, we are to experience Him for ourselves. God's fingerprints are imprinted on every one of us; it is for us to discover Him in the environment of our lives.

God sent angels to impart news to Mary and Joseph, spoke audibly to Samuel, and rescued Lot's family from Sodom, even when they didn't want to go. The Bible is full of testimonies of God's interactions with mankind that reveal different aspects of his multifaceted character.

God opened my eyes to see in the Spirit realm and to know how to engage His will. It's an asset in war to see the enemy advancing to call forth the guard. It's like getting a can of insect killer ready when you see a cockroach crawling. Would you rather live in an infested house but not know the problem, or would you rather see the problem and have an exterminator ready? Ignorance is not bliss; too many people have no idea when living in an infested house. We are called to see, sense, and respond, walking on the waves and keeping our eyes on Jesus.

We have the help of God's Holy Spirit, the great counselor given to us by God. Jesus told His disciples it was better that He ascend to the Father so the Holy Spirit would come and abide with us.

> Truly I tell you, it is for your good that I go away, for unless I go, the Helper will not come to you; but if I go, I will send him to you. (John 16:7)

Jesus told them the Holy Spirit would prove the world wrong about sin, righteousness, and judgment because the prince of this world, Satan, now stands condemned because of Jesus' victory on the cross.

> I have much more to say to you—more than you can now bear. But when the Spirit of Truth comes, he will guide you in all truth. (John 16:12)

After Jesus ascended to Heaven, He entered the locked room where the disciples were and stood among them, to their astonishment. Jesus showed them His hands and His side. The disciples rejoiced when they recognized it was their Lord. Jesus told them:

 "Peace be with you. As the Father has sent Me, I send you."

> Jesus breathed on them and told them to
> receive the Holy Spirit.

Jesus said we would do more incredible things in partnership with God's Holy Spirit, and the disciples received the infilling of the Spirit and performed many signs and wonders.

We are part of the great story, and it will only get more powerful as we prepare for the Lord's coming soon. There will be signs and miracles, resurrections from the dead, miraculous healings, and deliverances from demons. They are already happening through the body of Christ. Many people I know are raising the dead all over the world. Deaf ears are opening and blind eyes can see. These things will happen much more in the coming days. This is what Jesus instructed and empowered us to do.

After all, we belong to God's Kingdom, and it is a Kingdom of power and love.

WE MUST GET suited up in the armor of God, according to Ephesians 4. A warrior puts on his armor daily. The Bible does not tell us to defend our position but to storm the gates of Hell. This is the difference between being on the offense and not the defense. We are on the side of victory. But we need to step up and get in the game.

I was in a Bible study at a friend's house when I was overcome by a strong feeling of a threatening natural disaster coming to America. I saw the color brown and knew it had to do with an Earth-related storm like an earthquake or tornado. It was enormous and foreboding. *All* can prophesy and get a vision from God because we are all His children.

The group was in prayer, and something compelled me to share the premonition so we could pray. I couldn't shake the feeling and asked if we could pray. Some group members laughed at the strange request, but we prayed into the vision God had given me, asking God to spare lives and divert the storm to lessen its intensity.

The following day, I couldn't believe the news. There was a devastating tornado, reportedly the worst in a century. Nobody saw it coming, and no news or weather channel predicted it would happen. It descended with a fierce rage but then hardly touched ground—in fact, there were no fatalities and minor property damage in the four Midwestern states it stormed over. Newscasters on every television channel were perplexed and called it a miracle.

I knew God nudged me to pray, and I was so relieved that I did. I would have felt awful if I had not responded to God and heard the news later of a catastrophic storm. The tornados were not predicted and came about suddenly.

WHAT A MIRACLE that God chooses to use us to call for His will on Earth as on Heaven.

22

PARADE OF DEMONS

My eyes were opened in a terrifying way late one night to many spiritual critters outside my house on the street. I was awakened by a cacophony of loud voices marauding on the street corner below my bedroom window. It was no ordinary sound. A mob was laughing and loitering, slowly passing around the sidewalk corner below my window. I peered out the window, thinking it was a group of partying kids. Despite the loud voices outside my window, I was surprised to see no one outside. I prayed and pleaded for Jesus' blood to protect me and keep me hidden from the disturbance. God opened my eyes to show me what was making all that noise: it was a mob of demons of all sizes and shapes walking as if in a parade. There were large, short, fat, and blobby ones and tall, lanky creatures with their heads in the trees. They embodied malice. They glided without feet. The noisy mob lingered while I prayed in tongues in my room above.

After several hours of praying, I sensed the mob turn the corner and continue down the street. As if they were real people, I could hear the mob of demons moving down the road, riotously carousing. I tried to go back to sleep. The next day, I saw six police cars parked down the street in the direction the demons had turned. I had a horrible feeling in my gut. The cops wouldn't tell me anything except that the situation was under investigation. Later that afternoon, they were able to tell me of a murder that happened at one o'clock the night before. It was precisely where the parade of demons turned. Those evil spirits had been heading to the scene of a soon-to-be murder scene.

God taught me how important it is to do what He says and pray when He prompts. The Holy Spirit prompts us to take action, which we must do if we walk with God. Though it was a scary experience to see a gaggle of demons outside my window loitering and ambling, prayer interfered with Hell's intent to destroy lives that night.

The Bible tells us Jesus waits for all His enemies to be made His footstool. Jesus won the victory at the cross, gaining the keys and authority. But until authority is exercised, it is merely theoretical—a restraining order must be enforced to demonstrate its power. God backs us—we have the authority of Jesus to enforce the Father's will. Our cooperation with God assists in the Kingdom of Heaven manifesting on Earth. In the case of that evening, Satan likely planned for more violence, but God intervened.

The more we walk in the supernatural realm with Jesus, the more God will equip us for more significant battles. All are invited to walk in this level of authority in Jesus, and it takes a willingness to continually lay down one's will and turn one's ear to God. If we desire to be called a "friend of God" like Abraham, we must work toward a strong relationship through time and effort. There is no one more worthy of our time. May our response always be willing and ready, like Samuel in the Bible when he answered, "Hineni, Here I am," when the voice of the Lord stirs.

23

KNOTS IN A NET

The body of Christ needs to tune in to the Holy Spirit so we can flow and cooperate with God. Each of us is an integral part of the Body of Christ and has an important role.

A fishing net is made of many knots, and each one must be strong to catch the weight of the fish. First Corinthians tells us we are part of a body but should not desire to be a different function because our function is critical. If the whole body were an eye, where would the hearing be? Where would the sense of smell be if the whole body were hearing? But God placed the parts in the body just as He desired. If they were all one part, where would the body be? But they are, in fact, many parts, yet one body. Each of us is a knot in a fishing net, whether you are an extensive ministry or a single person. Whether young or old, strong or weak, influential or quiet, your prayers move mountains.

When we are not fishing with Jesus, we are to repair our nets to keep them strong.

Fishermen are constantly working to keep their nets strong. Rips and tears are expected and must be attended to. When drawn from the water, the net gets snagged on debris, sharp wood on the boat, and the force of weight. We can't rely on frayed nets to work correctly. It only takes one hole in an otherwise strong net, and the fish will escape.

Whether a net, a wall, or a sword, a good worker pays attention to the quality of the resources he needs for his work.

The Bible paints a beautiful picture of working together to repair. Nehemiah lamented that Jerusalem was not fortified. The wall was destroyed, and the safety of the city's inhabitants was at risk from enemy attack. Nehemiah led the men of the city to rebuild the wall. Each man repaired the section near him while holding a cement trowel in one hand and a sword in the other. The men ignored the taunts of mockers and continued building until their work was complete.

We work together and with purpose. People, churches, towns, and cities unite to build a massive fishing net for a mighty fish catch. In addition to the importance of its strength, each knot must be tethered well to its adjacent knots.

24

GOOD NEWS FOR ALL

There was a breaking news story about a small boy who was thrown over a balcony in a shopping mall by a stranger. He fell four stories over the ledge as people watched in horror. The boy survived with minor injuries and stated that angels caught him and gently placed him on the ground. When news crews asked him why he thought God would do that, he replied as if it was apparent.

"Because Jesus loves me."

We need that kind of trust. God loves us so much that He gave His only Son, Jesus, out of His love. Surely, you are beloved by God.

You are not only beloved but empowered by God. When the disciples returned to Jesus with joy because of their victory over demons, Jesus answered:

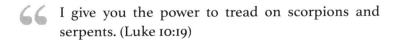 I give you the power to tread on scorpions and serpents. (Luke 10:19)

The prowling lion seeks to devour, and cobras try to strike the heel. They are down on the ground waiting to attack, but we are called above in the Spirit, in our rightful place seated with Jesus. They will never have victory because it belongs to Jesus for all eternity through His precious blood.

Jesus asked His disciples who they thought He was. He asked this question at Caesarea Philippi, located at the foothill of Mount Hermon. Mount Hermon was known as the birthplace of the Nephilim spirits and the location of Pagan worship, particularly the god Pan, who was half man and half goat. Infants were sacrificed in that location by being thrown against the rocks as an offering to Pan. Blue waters emerged in gushing waterfalls from that same mountain, Galilean rivers flowed, and millions of migratory birds rested. Jesus chose this location to announce that He is the living water and the Son of God.

Water is meant to have life, and that life is in Jesus.

Jesus drew a proverbial line in the sand as if to say, 'This far and no further, Satan, *for your Kingdom is coming down.*'

WHEN HE ASKED His disciples who they said He was, Simon Peter answered,

 "You are the Messiah, the Son of the Living God."

"Blessed are you, Simon bar Jonah, because flesh and blood did not reveal this to you, but My Father who is in Heaven."

Jesus told him that upon that revelation, He would build His church, and the gates of Hell would not prevail. The truth of Jesus as Messiah would be the foundation stone, not Peter. Only the Son of God could be this cornerstone that would serve as the structural key to God's plan.

Interestingly, Jesus referred to Peter as the son of Jonah,

showing that Peter would later identify with Jonah, resisting God's will to reach people deemed unworthy. Just as Jonah resisted bringing God's message to Nineveh, considering the Ninevites too sinful for God's mercy, likewise, Peter would be called to share the Good News with the first Gentile (non-Jewish) believer, showing that God's mercy extends to all people. Seeing what God was doing, Peter declared in Acts 10:34-36:

> I now understand that God does not show favoritism but accepts from every nation the one who fears Him and does what is right. You know the message God sent to the people of Israel, announcing the good news of peace through Jesus Christ, who is Lord of all.

The good news of Jesus was for all humanity. Through Jesus, Gentiles could be grafted into the family of God. Starting in Jerusalem, the Good News of Jesus would travel the globe to reach every nation and every tongue.

25

PEOPLE ARE FLAILING, HELP THEM

Titling this chapter made me laugh out loud, because it's simply how simple it is. We are to help people. The hope of Jesus gives us fire, power, and supernatural love, and His yoke is easy and light. We don't need long faces and coffin suitcases, like the Moravian missionaries years ago. We don't plod lifelessly toward death—we dance exuberantly in new life. If we have already died, then death has no power over us. We live a supernatural eternal life through Jesus.

I get this image of people in a rescue dinghy fleeing the Titanic while thousands are drowning; it's our responsibility in love to row back to them and pull them from the water. We must help them and not just look after our own interests. People are flailing. They are desperate for a touch from the Living God, and we are God's messengers appointed by Heaven.

Eric Ludy made a YouTube video, *The Gospel,* that powerfully portrays the Gospel message, emphasizing the hope that begins when sin's prison doors are opened through Jesus. But we are not to remain on the cell's cold cement floor, thanking God, for the door is wide open! We are to exit the cell and enter with the glorious light of the Kingdom of God. We respond to that freedom by sharing the great news with a desperate world.

AFTER RETURNING to the States from discipleship school, I visited a lung doctor who verified that I was healed from asthma. Since that witchcraft dagger was removed in the Spirit, I no longer needed all the medicines and machines I had dealt with for years. It was wonderful to have the confirmation of healing and to know that the Spirit of fear had left me.

At the doctor's that day, I noticed the receptionist was sick and wouldn't stop sneezing. So I said,

"Sounds like you're not doing too good."

"No," she replied, "I'm allergic to everything, and nothing helps."

"Have you ever been prayed for?"

"No."

"Would you like to be?"

"Yes!"

So we went into the supply room for her privacy, and I told her I pray in Jesus' name because He is the only one who saves.

"I know," she replied.

I went to pray a short prayer, holding her hands for God's power to flow. The power of the Holy Spirit fell on her.

"Do you feel that?" I asked her.

"Yes!"

"That's the presence of God. His Holy Spirit is here; can you feel it?"

"Yes! I'm shaking!"

She excitedly said this must be why she came to work today when she didn't want to. She asked me to pray for family members, and I led her to break generational curses. She was touched and healed, and it was awesome how God moved.

When we love like Jesus, we can't help but want to share with others. There are no longer chains that hold us. We've been set free to help others get free. Make yourself available for God's purposes. See what God will do with surrender. Though we are like ants on the back of an elephant, we are God's impetus for Him to loosen Hell's powers from people He desperately loves as He loves us. Jesus wants all to be saved and healed. We read in Matthew 9:25-38:

> Now Jesus was going around all the towns and villages, teaching in their synagogues, proclaiming the Good News of the Kingdom, and healing every disease and sickness. When He saw the crowds, He felt compassion for them because they were harassed and helpless, like sheep without a shepherd.

Then He said to His disciples,

> 'The harvest is plentiful, but the workers are few. Therefore, pray to the Lord of the harvest that He may send workers into His harvest field.'

Jesus' compassion focuses on a relationship with God and not religious dogma. Jesus' message was clear in the commission to His followers to make disciples of the world and set them free from bondage.

This story explains the simplicity of the Gospel. A man once told his daughter to clean her room. When he returned later that day, he checked on her progress. The room was a disaster. The girl sat smiling up at him.

"I thought I asked you to clean up your room," the father exclaimed.

"Oh, I have been memorizing what you said and invited friends later to discuss what you meant."

We need to step outside the walls of the church. Jesus has given us everything we need. We are partakers of His divine nature, having escaped the corruption that evil brought into the world. We share His compassion and lead people into a relationship with the Living God. We don't need a religion that makes manufactured systems of allegiance. God is relational, not distant. We can come into His presence freely through Jesus. In Him is abundant life and healing.

RELIGION IS the empty shell that is left when God leaves a building.

26

THE IN-BETWEEN SPACE

Being back in the States was a reverse culture shock. I felt like I had returned to Biblical Horeb, the in-between space where Elijah had hidden when he fled Jezebel and the Israelites had been encamped before arriving at Mount Sinai. I was back in a place stinging from my past sufferings—financial disaster, Duncan's passing, asthma, hospital trips, a sour breakup, and the passing of a friend. Emotions flooded back and threatened to undo the deep healing God had brought me through in the Bay of Plenty. That was now in the rearview mirror, and I faced an unknown expanse. Thankfully, God was close to my heart and strengthened me through the temptation to fall back into my old patterns. I had a promise from God from the year before; though I didn't know how it would manifest, I clung to it with every ounce of faith I had. Sorrow looks back. Worry looks around. But faith looks ahead.

Jesus tells us to seek first the Kingdom of God. I prayed for a quiet retreat for a week or so to be alone with God and process everything from the recent season. I didn't have money for a vacation. I couldn't go to my house, which was rented out to five single men at the time. I cried out to the Lord for somewhere to rest, and one day later my sister called to tell me friends offered their home to me for a week because they were vacationing the next day. If you don't think God has a sense of humor, the name of the street was Kiwi Lane, the official bird and name for residents of New Zealand. It was the perfect rest, journaling, praying, and seeking my next steps. God has faithfully provided housing wherever He has called me. He fuels faith into flame. He opens Heaven's doors when we hold our empty, surrendered hands high.

He speaks softly and leads us if we quiet ourselves to listen.

27

BURN THE PLOUGH, OFFER THE OXEN

When the prophet Elijah called Elisha to follow him (see First Kings 19), Elisha was busy ploughing the field with a team of twelve oxen. Elijah threw his cloak around him, which signified passing his mantle of anointing. Elisha ran after Elijah, wanting the anointing. But Elisha wanted to say goodbye to his parents first.

> Elijah answered, "Go back; what have I done to you?"

As new creations, we are God's children. Elisha figured it out. It wasn't so much that he couldn't say goodbye. He couldn't accept God's anointed call *and* return to life-as-usual. We have a choice to make. To follow God means letting go of the old ways and following one hundred percent. Elisha returned, but only so he could slaughter the twelve oxen, ignite the plough, and cook up the oxen meat on the fire. There was no Plan B. Then, he set out to follow Elijah. Any idea of a backup plan was wholly eradicated. There was no going home for him. He would be forever sold out for the call of God upon his life.

When Jesus was teaching to the crowds, His disciples came looking for Him to tell Him His mother and brothers were outside. His anointing as the Messiah, the beloved Son of God, was challenged by the status quo of what it means to be a Son of Man. But on which identity was Jesus to focus His attention? His reply made it clear. Jesus replied,

> "Who are My mother and My brothers?" Pointing to His disciples, He said, "Here are my mother and my brothers. For whoever does the will of my Father in Heaven is my brother and sister and mother." (Matthew 12:46-50)

I took a long bike ride along the Mohawk River to clear my head. Like Elisha, I was facing decisions for my future. Pedaling the canal banks, I took a break at a small cove under a canopy of trees. I looked at a pond with lily pads and reeds. A large white heron stood in the center of the pond. God's peace surrounded me. I sensed God speaking, quieting my anxious thoughts, and a waterfall kind of peace flooded my insides.

He told me I would be in Israel in October of that year.

That was five months away. I had no idea how, with whom, or why, but I clung to that word.

28

DOING WHAT YOU SAY, EVEN WHEN IT'S WEIRD

One Sunday morning, as church services ended, I saw an elderly man with the spirit of death hanging on him like a shroud. It startled me—I quietly prayed as I walked by him. I asked the Lord if He wanted me to command the spirit to leave, but God shared with me that the man would soon pass away. It was God's will, and He only wanted to allow me to see it. I had to learn to discern spirits and see them manifest to know who they were and whether God wanted me to act.

I realized that I wasn't the same person from the year before. I had a lot to learn from God.

I DIDN'T KNOW what to do in this gap of five months. I had no money or a place to live. God told me to trust Him and not to take a job. He told me to wait upon Him for the next steps. Everyone around me kept suggesting I get a job in the meantime. Cliches like 'God can't steer a parked car' circulated like broken records. But sometimes God wants us to park and wait. I wasn't about to return to life as usual unless everyday life was what God wanted. I knew deep down if I took any job, I'd be tempted to fall back into the comfort zone of an idol that threatened to resurrect called the American Dream.

It was a strange time in my life. I drove by my house often, wishing I could enjoy it. Cars and motorcycles filled the driveway and garage. Friends invited me to sleep on their couch. I stayed one month at one friend's, then moved to another couch for the following month. Couches are uncomfortable, and both families had little kids who woke early and played in the living room where I slept. God gave me exuberant grace, so I enjoyed those two months roughing it. I was walking by faith, and there is always grace for that.

During that time, a friend kept telling me she knew of an apartment for me to see. I kept telling her no thank you because I had no money to pay for an apartment and was following the mysterious leading of God to trust and wait on Him. She insisted, so I went to look at the place. A Christian single mother of two teenagers had a spare room and told me God told her to give it to me for free for as long as I needed. It had a bed, a kitchenette, a little sitting area, and a private bath. It was a significant improvement from couch-surfing, and with the generous conditions she offered, I knew it was the Lord.

Sometimes, you must tell your soul to come along with your spirit when we do not understand.

WE ARE a drop in His ocean, and we dance upon His waves.

29

ONE DREAM FOR ANOTHER

The season shifted. I moved in with my new friend and helped her around the house. I drove back and forth to my house to clear out my belongings and have estate sales. God wanted me to surrender the old dream for something new. I had to let go. I had a new bedroom set I'd just finished paying off before attending missions school. It represented something of an inheritance that I envisioned passing to my children someday. It was harder to part with that than the house. Buyers offered a fraction of my asking price, which made the sting worse. I wondered when God would stop asking me to surrender things or if this would be a perpetual requirement to live a life of faith. Finally, a couple bought the set.

I watched them load the five heavy pieces on a truck and drive my old dreams away. With no dog, no furniture, few possessions, and a house full of strangers, I was a little glum. I drove to a nearby cafe and had a bagel and coffee. A homeless man was begging outside. I invited him to be my guest and talked to him about Jesus. It was good to get my mind off myself. My next stop was the Apple store. I knew I needed a laptop for the coming phase of life. In God's perfect kindness, the cash I had from the furniture sale was precisely the right amount for a computer. Nothing is a coincidence with God.

In surrendering a dream that had meant so much, God would give His dream, which would be much better. Writing this book is a testimony of that provision that continues in its eleventh year of work. It was July, and God introduced me to a local missions organization to help me logistically. They asked what I sensed God calling me to next. I wasn't sure, except for the clear word that God told me I would be in Israel that October. I held that word in my heart for a year since God spoke it to me in New Zealand.

The pastors exchanged a knowing glance and told me they were sending a ministry team to Israel in October. Only God can arrange such things. I had two months to organize myself and seek the finances to go. For once, I wasn't worried because I had the word of the Lord.

And that was enough.

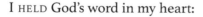

I held God's word in my heart:

> *"Go to Israel for three months.*
> *Take your guitar.*
> *I want to show you My Land.*
> *I want to show you My People."*

I argued about the guitar part. It's clunky and bulky to lug around. *Did I really have to carry it, Lord?* His reply was emphatic,

"Yes."

He repeated,

One Dream for Another

"Take your guitar, go for three months. I want to show you My Land. I want to show you My People."

I had the unquestionable and indisputable word of the Lord. I knew I needed to raise money. Wait a minute, no, I didn't. God was teaching me how to trust Him. That summer, trusting God brought more than I could have done on my own. Left on my own, I might have gotten tied down with a job and apartment and let my faith walk dwindle to a limp that fit into a packed life. I would have had my mountaintop experience and sailed on those winds the rest of my life, remembering when nostalgically. But I didn't want that. I wanted the rest of my life to be sailing on God's winds. Nothing less could satisfy.

I obeyed that weird word from God to not get a job, which unraveled the feathers of friends and family who thought that was strange since I was broke and in between seasons. It was a test because God wanted to see who I would listen to. When I passed the test, God showed me how much more He blessed me and others through that obedience. He brought new renters for the coming year. Things were falling into place.

God's plan is always better than anything we could imagine. When we let go of our desires and surrender to God to direct our lives as pleases Him, He can orchestrate so much more with us because we are thoroughly broken and beautiful in His hands. One hundred and twenty souls would soon be won for the Kingdom of God. It was beyond imagining, and only God could arrange it.

In early September, the two teenagers I was sharing a home with came home with news. Their Spanish teacher never showed up for the first day and quit without notice. The private Catholic school was without a Spanish teacher. I told their mom I'd been a Spanish teacher on and off for twenty years. Their mom asked if I would consider the work. I prayed, and God released me, so I met the principal that afternoon, informing her I was leaving for Israel the next month and could only fill in as a teacher until then.

I got the job and had the weekend to prepare ten levels of Spanish lesson plans for kindergarten through grade eight middle school level. There were no plans or books in the room to use; I had to get sorted fast. God rained favor on me: they paid me a bonus and prep time, and the money I needed for a ticket to Israel was raised with that three-week assignment. More than that, it was a 'God assignment' that exceeded my provisional need. I was about to discover what God was working for me to do for Him.

Sitting at the teacher's desk Monday morning, I was excited to meet my pupils. My notes were in hand. My books were organized. I wanted to be the best teacher and started striving for the first week. A friend gently reminded me I was on God's assignment, so I should ask Him what He brought me there for. It was more than teaching Spanish. So, I started having fun with my lessons, bringing my guitar and teaching numbers, colors, verbs, and nouns. As the history teacher brought her students to my classroom, she told them they should ask about my life as a missionary since they were studying missionaries in history class. The principal assured me I could share openly and pray. I had an open door.

The kids started asking me questions.

"How does God provide for you? Does money fall from the sky? How do you hear God's voice? Does He speak out loud?"

There was so much excitement. I decided to allow ten minutes to answer their questions at the end of class so we could still do Spanish. They watched the clock like hawks.

"Teacher," they said, "It's time."

So, every day, I answered questions and told them Bible stories. I told them about Jacob falling in love with Rachel. I told them about Gideon's army and Joseph in the pit. I told them the story of Abraham and Isaac and the ram in the thicket that God provided. I shared stories from the book of Acts, miracles of Jesus, and pilgrimages of early disciples. I shared the story of the Exodus from Egypt. Every day, we saved ten minutes before the end of class for me to share. Their little hands went up and the questions flew. I never had such attentive eager clock watchers.

We got onto the subject of the Holy Spirit. I was teaching about Jesus and how He died for our sins. On Friday, I asked the fifth graders,

"Would you like to pray and ask Jesus into your heart?"

We had been so fired up with Bible stories that it was a natural next step.

They were excited and agreed. Standing in a circle, thirty students prayed and invited Jesus into their hearts. We prayed, asking Jesus to forgive our sins, cleanse us in His blood, and live in our hearts. Dozens of faces beamed like angels, and I realized God's purpose for me in that school. I would have missed this fantastic opportunity if I had ignored God's instruction months earlier. That is the reward for submission to Jesus. I was thrilled to see the immediate fruit that would ripple to generations to come. But there was more blessing to unfold.

"Did you know that when you accept Jesus into your heart, He promises a helper from God for the rest of your life? That helper is the Holy Spirit. He is a gift from God, and He will dwell with you always. Even if you can't see Him, you can feel Him and know He's by your side."

The room was transfixed.

"Would you like to meet and invite the Holy Spirit into your life?"

The room buzzed with excitement. I continued.

"He is like a quiet wind—You may feel Him, and you may not. But know He is always with you. He is the promise of Heaven, the deposit of our inheritance in eternity with Jesus."

"Oh yes!" they exclaimed. "We would like that."

"Put your hands before you and turn your palms facing Heaven. I'll invite the Holy Spirit into the room. You may feel something, and you might not. He will be there whether you feel Him or not."

I led a short prayer and invited the Holy Spirit to come and dwell with them.

"Come, Holy Spirit," I prayed. "Show these children that you are real, that you are here, and that you love them so much."

The room filled with excitement. A pillar of electric energy fell into the room. The children exclaimed.

"I can feel it! Do you feel it?"

God's presence was thick in the room.

"The Holy Spirit is God. We read about Him in the Bible. He will help you as your friend and counselor through every battle of your life, and He will never leave you."

Just then, the bell rang and class was dismissed. As a room of fifth-graders spilled out to the hallway, they passed the sixth-graders waiting to enter the room.

"Be sure she prays with you at the end of class! You must experience this awesome thing!"

The hall filled with excited voices sharing how their hands tingled and felt the presence of God. The sixth-graders watched the clock on the wall.

Then Heaven broke loose, and we prayed and invited Jesus into our hearts and the Holy Spirit to dwell with the children. The bell rang again, and the seventh grade was waiting at the door. So that Friday afternoon went. All fourth, fifth, sixth, seventh, and eighth-grade students were born again in Jesus.

Altogether, one hundred and twenty children invited Jesus Christ to be their Lord and Savior and received the outpouring of the Holy Spirit. It was marvelous.

I went home that afternoon elated.

As I drove home with my heart full, I started to worry about

One Dream for Another

what I would face Monday morning after the students shared the experience with their families. I prayed and fasted all weekend, and friends rallied around me in prayer.

I arrived early to school Monday morning. The students came bustling in, and a long queue stood at my desk with excited animation to tell me their news.

"Teacher, you won't believe what happened this weekend!"

One after another, they shared testimonies of how they shared their Friday encounters with their families and prayed at home for parents and siblings to be born again. I couldn't believe my ears.

"Teacher," one girl whispered, "Would you pray for my uncle who drinks too much? I want God to heal him."

"Teacher," another girl said, "I prayed with my grandma, and she invited Jesus into her heart too!"

Story after story after story. I asked the Lord for help. We continued Spanish lessons with ten minutes every class to pray. I taught them how to pray and not depend on me to pray for them. Each day, they watched the clock, each tender heart coming alive, nurtured by God. On my last day, the students handed me drawings with hearts and pictures from Bible stories we had learned and said how much they would miss me. That last week, I taught them a song about a donkey wearing clothing in different colors so we could learn colors and nouns. It was a snappy little tune; we all sang while I played guitar, and they colored little donkey drawings. I now have dozens of donkey drawings, his yellow scarf, black hat, red jacket, and little pointy tap shoes, all signed with love as a farewell gift. The heart can melt from love so easily. All this and Heaven too. This is just a fraction of the love God has.

I am overwhelmed by how God opens doors. One hundred and twenty children will never be the same. What an honor from the Lord to be the fortunate gardener to nurture God's tender children, to see them sprout in overflowing life through

Him and leap through the paddock like sheep with their Shepherd. Let the little children come to Jesus.

I walked out of school that day with my head held high and a pile of donkey drawings with scrawled prayers and well-wishes gathered under my arm. I would have enjoyed staying there, but I was going to Israel—the trip was days away. I moved out of the apartment with the woman and her two kids. I loaded the car again and again, bringing things to anyone who wanted, overwhelmed by the volume four walls of a house could contain. Things were thrown in large bags and driven off anywhere people could be blessed.

So it began. What started with a girl longing for the wild unknown became the girl in an empty big house with nothing but a prayer and one word on her lips—Israel. What would God have for me there?

Israel was an unexpected yearning in my heart. I saw its significance on every page of the Bible behind a mysterious veil of intrigue, and I was excited to see what God had for me next.

"I want to show you My land. I want to show you My people."

I had a vision of a star in the sky—a blue and white star.

"THIS IS THE JEWISH LIGHT. Go to My beloved—the Jewish People, for this is where you belong."

30

ISRAEL—THE HEART OF GOD

I flew to Israel for a three-month faith journey that began with ten days of touring with an Orthodox Rabbi and a Christian Pastor. After the initial tour, I did not know what to do or where to go. I just knew God told me to go for that length and that He would show me.

The tour was magnificent, with times of fellowship and learning between Christians and Jews. We sat in Bible studies with Rabbis; we chopped vegetables for Shabbat meals with Jewish women as they taught us traditional songs. We ate bountiful meals in their homes and played with their children. We prayed at the Kotel, the closest where the Holy of Holies stood in the Biblical Temple. We walked through the Old City and the City of David through water shafts and tunnels built by Hezekiah to divert water from the Gihon Spring.

I met half a dozen Orthodox Jewish rabbis in one week, sharing life, stories, and teachings. Is this not the hand of God? He showed me His beautiful people with shining souls warming quickly to us despite generations of hurt in the name of Christianity. As the Bible says, we were truly coming together; it felt so holy and special. We mourned the holocaust at Yad Vashem with our new friends and got to know a man born in a displaced persons camp whose parents both lost their partners and families to the Holocaust. So many moving conversations and meaningful connections were made every day. The time with my new Jewish friends was sacred. After ten packed days, I waved goodbye to the group leaving, standing alone on a street corner in Jerusalem. I had no idea what I would do next.

What happened next was undoubtedly the hand of God. The next day, I got an invitation to a gathering of global Christian leaders. I had heard there was an annual gathering in Jerusalem but had no connections, nor did I know when in the year it took place. Wouldn't you know? It started the following day, and somehow, the announcement was sent to me, but I had no idea who it was from or how they knew me.

I attended the five-day event and met new friends from around the world who love Israel and teach their nations the importance of standing as Christians with Israel and the Jewish People. I also met national leaders—Eskimo Inuit and Romanian Gypsy Christians, First Nations leaders from North America, Norwegian, Finnish, and Ukrainian believers, and many more.

I soon found out why God told me to bring my guitar. A man from Galilee talked about how Tiberias was one of the nation's holiest cities—he prayed that God would send people there to worship God over the geographic atmosphere. My spirit jumped. God told me to bring my guitar for this trip! I knew that was my next assignment from God. So I settled into a small motel in Tiberias, praying on the rooftop over the Sea of Galilee. I prayed, fasted, and worshiped on the rooftop, looking over the luscious region for the first time and feeling like I'd been there before. There was a feeling of completeness and peace as if the atoms I needed to inhale could only be received in Eretz Zion.

I wanted to reach the Sea of Galilee and touch the water. It was difficult because my motel was on a steep hill several miles above the sea. I braved the walk and looked for an access point to the water. There was a small path to the water behind a hotel. The majestic water of so many Bible stories glistened before me. I inhaled deeply and was about to put my feet in when a dark cloud suddenly came over my head. I became confused and discouraged in an instant. Thoughts attacked me, telling me I was out of God's timing, God wouldn't take care of me, God was angry with me, and that I went to Israel for selfish reasons. It was Satan berating me with powerful doubt and lies; my head reeled. Was I really here on a selfish trip? Did God really call me? My mind was foggy. I wanted to leave at once.

I turned away, feeling unworthy to be in such a holy place. A pure white heron soared over my head, making several large loops above me. He landed by my right side, putting his tall, limber legs in the water.

At once, the dark cloud over me vanished.

I looked long at the heron, then walked one foot after the other into the Sea of Galilee as time lost all meaning.

Jesus deals swiftly with our enemies when we walk according to God's will. I knew those were lies, but they still had tremendous power over me. I needed Jesus at that moment, and He was already there, ready to deliver me.

The waters were refreshing. My spirit felt reborn. Something about water feels timeless—as if the molecules wetting my skin were the same drops witnessing miracles from two thousand years ago.

The next day, I ran into a Ukrainian family I had met the week before in Jerusalem. We spent the day at Capernaum and the Mount of Beatitudes. God reminded me that I'd never lack for community when I abide with Him. It was wonderful to be with people.

One of my favorite things was visiting different lookout

points around the Sea of Galilee to pray. I spoke into the winds and declared the Word of God. It's hard to explain the feeling of standing over a region where so much history happened, where Jesus taught. For ten days, I prayed over the Galilee. My friend from the conference checked in with me every day to see how I was doing. I assured him I was fine. On the ninth day, I sensed my assignment from God was finishing because His cloud of glory was shifting me. It was then I met nine Christians who invited them to join them in Haifa. Their medical ministry ship was drydocked in Haifa. They came to Israel from Russia, Germany, Ecuador, Mexico, Argentina, Sweden, Iran, and Finland. I served with them for the next two weeks, leading the group in worship in Nazareth while we all talked with Arab teens. We worshiped also at Mount Carmel, where Elijah faced the prophets of Jezebel. There were many opportunities to lift worship to God, and I understood why He wanted me to bring my guitar.

31

ANGEL ON THE BUS

I was alone on a bus from Haifa to a Messianic church an hour away. Some American friends attended that church but didn't seem happy to see me. After service, I tried to mingle but felt out of place. I wanted to crawl under a rock, and suddenly, all the craziness that I was doing traveling solo around Israel hit me like a ton of bricks. I felt overwhelmingly alone. After failed attempts to connect and feeling rejected by my friends, I went to the bus stop to wait for the bus.

After twenty minutes, the bus came, and dozens of church congregants filled the rows. I found a seat by myself and wanted to cry. I put my head down, looking toward the window and fighting back tears. A woman nodded to ask if she could sit next to me. I half smiled my consent, although I didn't want to be bothered. I was reading a book called *Angels Among Us*, a collection of angelic encounter stories. The woman pointed at the book so I could show her the title. She pointed at the word 'angels' and then pointed at herself with a bright smile. She put her arm around me, her eyes glowing with joy. The bus ambled down the mountain along curving streets. She kept looking over at me and smiling. I tried to have a conversation, but she didn't speak English. Glancing at my book, pretending to read, I started to enjoy this mysterious woman who kept hugging me every few minutes. My sadness was gone. I was filled with a deep and satisfying peace. As the journey continued, I wanted to take a photo of us to remember this unexpected encounter. Lifting my cell phone, I gestured to ask if I could. She became alarmed and waved her hands—no, no, no. I put my phone away.

We approached the city and she kept glancing at me and laughing to a secret I didn't know. She gestured goodbye, saying she was about to get off the bus and hugged me tightly. She departed.

The bus pulled away, and I craned to see where she was going. The woman was nowhere in sight. I scanned the area thoroughly but she was gone. It dawned on me that I had just encountered an angel to encourage me. The love and joy of the Father flooded me, and doubt and fear left. I could feel God's great pleasure in me and that I was walking this faith journey alone with Him.

 Do not neglect to show hospitality to strangers— for in doing so, some have entertained angels without knowing it. (Hebrews 13:2)

32

ANCIENT PATHS

God continued to take care of me. I started getting nervous when my money ran out; I had less than one hundred dollars several times on the Israel trip, but then a miracle would happen, and an anonymous person would deposit money in my account. One day, my account went from zero to one thousand dollars, and I did not know who made such an extravagant gift. My faith was being tested, and I started to relax and trust that my needs would be met continually. The Bible tells us not to worry about tomorrow because God is faithful in caring for us when we lean on Him.

I was halfway through my three-month faith journey to Israel, and the team was leaving the following week. For eighteen days, I ministered with my nine new friends throughout Haifa, Nazareth, Tel Aviv, and Tiberias. Their last stop was to be Jerusalem for a week, and since they'd not been there and I had, they asked me to lead them around. It was a joy to navigate the winding streets of the Old City and show them the highlights I had only discovered weeks earlier. I was a fledgling guide with a contagious passion for the city and people.

I introduced the group to my new Jewish friends, who

graciously received the large group at their Shabbat table. It was extraordinary to realize I knew none of those people the month before and discover that God supernaturally connected me with many people and places in a way I never imagined. God was bringing Jews and Gentiles together to break bread together. It was so special to share our faiths deeply with one another, both Christians and Jews, as friendships budded on the mutual worship we shared for the same God.

On our team was a German man who prayed for an elderly Holocaust survivor. We wept as he washed her feet in a large basin, asking her forgiveness for what she endured.

One day, as I walked alone on the sidewalks of Jerusalem, a stranger approached and told me in Spanish.

"This is your home. Esto es tu casa."

I watched the man keep walking as I wondered. How did he know I spoke and understood Spanish? The Lord whispered in my heart a vague shadow of Spanish Jewish heritage from centuries earlier. It was a mystery, but I couldn't shake the feeling that I was home everywhere I went in Israel and that my ancestors walked the same ancient paths.

Another time, I was walking through downtown Jerusalem and saw two young women in front of me. One of them had the spirit of death on her—I could see it perched on her shoulder like a black cloud. I asked the Lord what He wanted me to do and asked if He wanted me to help her, that He'd get her friend away from her so I could talk. I also needed Him to remove the two friends with whom I was walking from me. I knew it had to be just me and the one woman. As you might expect, all three friends got distracted by shopping in different directions in the blink of an eye, and I could walk beside the young woman. I made small talk. She was visiting the weekend from London on her first trip to Israel. I told her I could see things and could tell her what I saw on her. With her permission, I told her I saw a heavy grief, like a weighty burden, lingering around her. I asked if I could pray for her, and she agreed again.

I specified that I pray in the name of Jesus, to which she also agreed. So, quietly walking beside her and taking her arm in mine like old friends, I commanded the spirit to leave her in Jesus' name. It left her at once. I saw it fly away like a cloud of smoke. In an instant, the woman curled over in sobs and hysterics, feeling relief from the heaviness she had carried. She explained the circumstances and had lost someone close to her recently, and we talked and prayed and hugged. At the perfect moment, not a moment sooner, all three friends came rushing back and were full of questions about what had just happened. The young woman's friend was astonished and delighted because she knew the grief her friend had carried. Freedom was won that afternoon because Jesus loves everyone and wants everyone to be free and unburdened!

This is the God we delight in. I could minister to the woman in a way that only benefited her and did not disturb her. I'm thrilled that God allowed me to see that foul spirit so the woman could taste freedom.

33

SNOW PRAYER

God's heart is enormously in love with the Jewish People and Israel. At Synagogue one Shabbat, a Jewish woman grabbed my hand to dance with the women as we celebrated a recent wedding of one and an engagement of another. There was so much joy and community. What unexpected opportunities to celebrate life. On another Shabbat, twelve Orthodox Jews asked me what I was doing in Israel, with no money or plan but the 'Word of the Lord.' They asked me to explain. I shared stories of God's miraculous provisions and how He was showing me His land and His people. I had a very attentive audience. They were excited to hear how God was providing for me and how I had listened to His voice telling me where to go and what to do.

One young man, Mordecai, lamented that he wished he heard God's voice.

"You can," I told him.

Mordecai asked me, half joking, if I would ask God for a snowy day next week because he didn't want to go to work. I knew there was a deep longing to see if God would respond in a tangible way. I replied I'd ask God on his behalf, but whatever happened, God cares about the details of our lives. He pressed me to ask, so I pressed him to be more specific.

"What day would you like to miss work?"

Tuesday was his thoughtful answer.

Later that night, I asked God to show how real He was and that He answered prayer; I asked God if He would bring a snow day so Mordecai could miss work on Tuesday. More than that, I asked God to show Mordecai that He was real and cared. It was early fall, and snow rarely fell in Jerusalem, even in winter, and not before.

The forecast was to be warm and mild for the next week. Still, I prayed.

The next day, everything changed. Jerusalem buzzed with news of a sudden storm coming.

I laughed out loud in surprise and felt tremendous awe for God. I couldn't wait to see Mordecai's reaction. The news reported that a severe storm was imminent—a whopper of a blizzard—and was expected Monday night. People were advised to stock up on food. The stores were packed. The weather sharply turned, and the city closed for the storm.

Tuesday was a snow day.

I wanted to see Mordecai and get his reaction. I am positive he was astounded. I didn't see him again, but I'm sure he knew God attended to our prayers. His specific prayer was answered.

GOD IS attentive to the small things. The details in a blade of grass, the imprints of fingertips, and the velvet petals on a rose demonstrate the heart of the Creator. I remembered a morning years earlier when I saw a baby deer nibbling on the grass too close to a busy highway. Cars rushed fast, and the deer was too close to traffic. A line of thick evergreen was recessed a hundred yards away. My heart throbbed for its safety, and I prayed.

"Jesus, I know you care about the little things. Protect that deer and lead it away from the highway."

At once, the fawn lifted its head from grazing on the grass and looked up curiously. Then, as if being led by a person, it turned 180 degrees backward to disappear into the safety of the thick evergreens away from the highway. God immediately answered my prayer as I drove along the busy road.

He really does care about little things. He cares much more about people like Mordecai, like you and me, who want to know and believe He is involved and cares.

If He cares about sparrows and lilies in a field, don't you think He cares much more for you?

34

VISION OF A MOUNTAIN

We are all running up the same mountain toward God's presence. We cannot see what God is doing on the other side of the mountain, just like on the far side of the moon. We only know to pursue Him, to desire His Presence, and to draw toward His face. What He is doing beyond our perspective is not pertinent to our journey upward to the apex. Mountain climbers face resistance but persist in their endeavor to reach the reward of the view from the top.

I had a vision of a small, pointed hill coming from the surface of the dirt. It was no bigger than a bump at first. It was engulfed with a swarm of black flies and gnats that circled it like a ring. The flies were demonic oppression around God's people on the mountain of the Lord. While the hill was small, the ring seemed to overtake it.

I watched the vision unfold, and the hill rose from the earth. It became larger and larger, like an iceberg emerging. When I thought it was fully grown, it continued to grow. It became a mighty mountain, bigger than any mountain. With a fixed rhythm it ascended, constant like a ticking clock and steady as an elevator. As the mountain grew more prominent, the ring of flies persisted in a circle; however, it shrank compared to the growing mountain and looked puny, like a gnat you swat away.

Along the side of the mountain were multitudes of people climbing to the top. These were followers of Jesus. Some were slow, and some were sprinting; some were old and feeble and needed help. Others were young. If a person stumbled, there was a quick hand to help. Everyone had the same objective: to get to the top of the mountain. No one was offended that some people sprinted past.

No one tried to pull anyone down. It was not a race. I could see only half the mountain and wondered what was on the other side. There was a general hum of curiosity among the climbers to know what was on the other side. When the people finally reached the top, the view was great. They were above the ring of pestering flies and gnats. Only then could they see down the other side of the mountain. There were enormous multitudes of Jewish people climbing the other side. Old and young, fast and slow, all on the same mission to reach the top of the mountain. Not until everyone reached the top could they see the complete picture of what God was building.

AND THEY WERE all on the mountain of God.

35

AN OPEN DOOR

I lived with my new Jewish friends in their home in downtown Jerusalem for two weeks. I met these warm families a month earlier, and they invited me to stay with them for two weeks.

I loved getting to know their family and learning about Jewish customs. They wanted to know more about my faith journey to Israel. Hanukah was coming; it was fun for me to learn about it and celebrate with them. For eight nights, the windows lining the cobblestone streets illuminated brighter as the number of candles increased. We ate sugary donuts with friends who dropped in for festivities.

They told me I was the first Christian they'd gotten to know, and I had many questions. It was such a beautiful time to learn from and love one another like family. This became a solid foundation for building long-lasting friendships and introducing more Christians to befriend and learn from our Jewish brothers and sisters.

Toward the end of the second week, I was curious about where God would move me next. I knew I was to stay the remaining five weeks of my journey in downtown Jerusalem to lead worship and prayer sessions for the Lord. There was a prayer tower where Christians from many nations came to pray for the peace of Jerusalem. It was modeled after Isaiah 62:6-7:

 "I have set watchmen on your walls, Jerusalem, who will never slumber nor sleep. You who call on the Lord, give yourselves no rest, and give Him no rest till he establishes Jerusalem and makes her the praise of the earth."

After forty hours of singing every worship song I knew the first week, I sat quietly, all alone, and wondered what I would sing next to worship God. I flipped open my Bible and started singing the Word of God with whatever melody was in my heart. I felt God sigh with gladness that I would finally pour my soul into Him and not just regurgitate someone else's beautiful songs, but not personal to me. God said,

"Finally, you're going to sing from your heart."

It was liberating to sing freely, because that is what prayer and worship are—a fresh conversation and not a Hallmark card that someone else wrote.

I was looking for a place to rent for a month and couldn't find anything due to the busy Christmas season. A hotel room was too expensive; I was down to a hundred dollars in the bank again that had to last until God provided more. I prayed and looked, with my new friends making calls in Hebrew for me. As my visit with the family neared its end, my host was getting nervous that I hadn't found a place to go. Even the hostels were occupied as it was nearing Christmas, and tourists were coming in droves. I didn't have enough money for one night in a hotel. I prayed and asked God to show me what to do.

The day before my final day with the family, a woman

from the prayer room messaged me and invited me to stay with her on the far side of town for a fee. I learned that that part of the city was not as safe for a single woman, and I wanted to be more central to my friends and prayer room—I didn't have the peace from God to accept her offer. But I ignored that warning, reluctantly accepting since no other offer surfaced.

That night, I wrestled a sleepless night with a strong sense that I should not go there, even though people suggested this seemed the logical door as it was the only open one. God was training me again to trust His voice above every other. Even when I could not see what was next in my journey, I needed to follow the voice I was learning so clearly as God led me. In the morning, as I sat with the Rabbi's wife, I told her I had no peace and had to decline that offer, even though I wasn't sure what I would do.

"Where will you go?"

"I don't know, but I trust God will somehow provide something."

I called and turned down the offer I had accepted the night before from the woman in the prayer room. My friend sat at my side and listened intently. As I hung up the phone, I sat with her silently; not a word was spoken for ten minutes as we both sipped our coffees, and I wondered if I had done the right thing.

Then my phone rang. Someone else from the prayer room called me and offered me an apartment. A couple was traveling, and the offer was for their apartment the next day. They would be overseas for five weeks, exactly when I needed housing. They would return the day after I was to return to the States. It couldn't have been more perfectly arranged by God. Plus, they didn't want any money for rent except a modest hundred dollars to help with utilities. That was all the money I had and, again, was the hand of God. Also, their apartment was adjacent to the prayer room just two blocks away and as central to everything as you could imagine.

My friend listened to my phone call, and we were both speechless. Only God could do this.

The miracle was born after I allowed the wrong door to close without knowing the next door. I had to turn down that first offer and trust in God. His peace was leading me, and I had to listen to it. God's peace would lead me above worldly logic to the natural eye. He knows our needs and wants us to put our faith in Him, for His plan is always best.

God provided so much better than the first offer. The second place's location, timing, and price were superior to the first. And although the first woman had good intentions in offering, it simply was not the will of the Father that I go there, for whatever reason only He knows. It was my job to obey and let His will lead me. It truly is fantastic when we put our trust in God.

We don't see what God wants to do for us when we limit God. On that faith journey to Israel, He freed me from the spirit of poverty that had taunted me for too long, telling me I wasn't worthy of crumbs from God's banqueting table. In fact, for most of the early weeks of the trip, I scrimped the little money I had, eating a lot of pita and hummus because I was afraid to run out of funds. I only had a debit card, so I had no fallback plan if the money wasn't in the bank.

As the weeks passed, I learned to trust a little more and hope a little higher. I sang of God's goodness in the prayer room, but did I believe it for my life? It was becoming apparent that God cared about my needs, and they exceeded the practical and even satisfied my longings. My wallet would not dictate what I could do with God each day. As we walk the exciting faith walk with Him, He provides the path for our feet one step at a time. We have much to learn about God's ways, His Kingdom, and His order of doing things.

An Open Door

The following day, I turned the key to open the door of my new apartment. Before me was a stunning apartment, and as my mind processed the goodness of God's provision, I glimpsed how God loves me and cares about every little thing. This would be my home for my remaining five weeks in Israel. God did what He said and showed me His land and His people. The guitar was necessary for the journey, so God told me to bring it despite my protesting.

I returned later that year to live in Jerusalem for two more years. His plans unfolded for me as I took one step at a time. For all the planning I could have done on my own, there is no way I could have written a better, more colorful three months than to let God weave the threads together and shape my future steps through the connections I could never have made on my own.

36

WORSHIP BREAKER

Worship is a weapon that breaks chains from the enemy. God is enthroned in the praises of His people. When we worship God, the battle shifts. Whether in a deep valley or a high mountain, we can fight the powers of darkness by worshiping the Living God. He fights for us while He gathers us under His wing, as written in Psalm 91, warring with passion for His Name's sake.

We have many weapons, like faith, trust, rest, and joy. These weapons defy the enemy's armies and unravel their schemes. When God prepares a table for us in the presence of our enemies, our cups overflow as darkness looks on from outside the window.

Worship is more than adoration of God. Worship must be at the frontline of every battle. The shofars blow, and God's Name is lifted. Jericho's walls came crumbling down. The trumpets and shouts that circled Jericho were worship weapons. The book of Judges says praise goes first into battle because it carries the breaker anointing. Psalm 129 talks about the high praises of God. Psalm 24 tells us we are the gates the King of Glory enters when we lift high praise to the Lord, proclaiming who God is and interceding for God's will to be accomplished. Heaven is voice-activated. Psalm 103, verse 20, talks about how our sound partners with God's heart. Judah goes first. Judah is the *yodah*, the praise of God. The release of sound shifts atmospheres.

Worship is not just a composition of musical notes. Our voices are instruments and weapons when we declare who our God is. We tell God how awesome He is, and as we declare it to the atmosphere, the enemy hears it and loses rank. It is like manna for God's angels—like incense before God's throne. David worshiped as he threw stones at Goliath, declaring that no one defy or mock his God—the mighty God of Heaven. His rocks hit the mark to bring down a giant because his faith directed them with the hand of God for victory.

Scripture says that the rocks and trees worship God. How is it possible that creation praises God? What does it look like for a hill to dance? For a rock to sing? For an animal to glorify God? All creation praises each in its unique sound and energy given by the Creator. Worship cannot be contained on a church stage or in a recital's grand hall. It is a fluid-moving power. We sing louder than the waves. We sway our branches like sequoias in praise. Rumble your waves more deafening than the ocean because God is worthy of all praise. To be a breaker upon the rock is to make a lasting ripple that never ends, causing the sand to swirl and dance.

We worship God through our actions when we step out of our comfort zone and trust Him even when it doesn't make sense. Gideon worshiped God when he allowed God to whittle his small army of 32,000 down to 300, going against 120,000 Midianites. Even though his numbers were small, God said they were still too large. God instructed Gideon to march into battle with torches, pitchers, swords, and trumpets (see Judges 7). What would that look like today? Guitars and flashlights and shouts of praise? God did what He told Gideon, giving him victory and delivering the Midianites into Gideon's hands. We do not boast of our strength. We know that with God's help, we can do what He sets us to do. It is for God's glory and not ours. Blessed is the one who trusts the Lord, whose confidence is in the King of Heaven.

Another way worship is a weapon is when we disregard what people may think of us and worship God with zeal, like King David dancing in the streets. David defied protocol and was ridiculed because he worshiped God and danced zealously in humble dress, not in his regal robes. He didn't care what anyone thought—he was worshiping God. His wife, Michal, Saul's daughter, was demoted by God for chastising her husband for his seeming lack of decorum.

When David built his palace in the vulnerable valley instead of the mountaintop, he declared that his help came from God. This is worship. Every other ruler would build a fortress and palace upon a high place; David knew that only God deserved the high place. He was a man after God's heart.

In Second Samuel, chapter 22, David sang to the Lord in praise of delivering him from his enemies and Saul's hand. David called the Lord his rock, fortress, deliverer, refuge, shield, stronghold, savior, and the horn of his salvation. He continued to praise God for saving him when death's torrential waves overwhelmed him.

> The Lord lives! Praise be to my Rock! Exalted be my God, the Rock, my Savior! I will praise You, Lord, among the nations; I will sing the praises of Your Name. (v.47, 50)

When we don't take a job because God tests our obedience when the world thinks we're strange, that is worship. When the widow gives the prophet Elijah her last bread and nothing left to eat, that is worship. No matter the situation, we heed the voice of the Lord and respond in faith. As a result, the widow was blessed with more than enough food for her family. One hundred children receive Jesus as Lord in a Catholic school. God calls David a man after God's own heart.

There is a time to war, and there's a time to adore. Worship wins wars in the heavens, tearing down demonic strongholds. God sits enthroned upon the worship and wields His strong arm against the foe. When we sit at Jesus' feet in adoration of who He is, we are worshiping. There is a season for contemplative and breaker worship, like detail-painting bone china or smashing a wall with a hammer. God sends different kinds of winds, from zephyrs to cyclones. A heartbeat can be calm or racing; the sea can be stormy or motionless as glass—different rhythms, each for their purpose, all beating under the heartbeat and direction of God.

His love is the whisper in your heart and the river in your pulse.

In Hebrews 11, we read of men and women who, through faith, conquered Kingdoms and gained what was promised. They shut the mouths of lions, quenched flames, and escaped the sword's edge. Their weakness was turned into strength. Do you want to be like those water walkers? Now is the time for God's next move, releasing extravagant water walkers who respond to God's voice with radical faith. When we comprehend how much greater are those with us than against us, our courage will rise.

In Second Kings 6:16, the prophet Elisha declared:

> Do not be afraid. The army that fights *for* us is larger than the one against us.

37

THE UNDERGROUND CHURCH

The prayer tower sometimes had dozens of visitors; other times, it was empty with just me alone, worshiping God. I began preferring the aloneness, those more intimate times with the Lord. One day, after a four-hour worship watch in the prayer room, an occultist pretended to be a believer and sat in the prayer room while I worshiped God.

I knew he was a warlock, a servant of Satan. He wanted to curse the prayer movement in Jerusalem. After I finished the prayer watch, he approached me with strange questions I did not answer. I saw the green shroud of demonic infestation all over his body. He was not fooling me. Then I saw his mangled hand, so I offered to pray for him that God would touch and heal him. The moment I felt his hand, the man shot backward six feet as if punched in the gut. He stood up, confused, and gathered his composure. That was the power of God in me that hit him. He looked at me strangely but wasn't ready to leave. I knew he was on assignment to collect information and try to curse what God was blessing.

I asked if he was a follower of Jesus, and he mumbled something incoherent but did not answer. I already knew the answer. I knew who he was. I asked if he had ever been involved in the occult, and he mumbled something about a little but long ago. I already knew he was a high-ranking servant of darkness. He tried to get information from me about prayer groups. He failed. Then, in a low, dark voice, he told me,

"I know you are part of the underground church."

I knew I was because God told me. I did not need to hear that from a demon and remained tight-lipped. As I led him to the door, I realized I was on the enemy's target—he knew who I was. As I walked home, I mustered my New York grit to lose someone in a crowd, scoping over my shoulder to be sure I wasn't followed as I zigzagged the streets. Getting home, I bolted the door and prayed. It was interesting to learn what the enemy revealed; I knew the prayer movement was a threat.

Twenty minutes later, the warlock was inside my apartment, standing in front of me in bodily form. He stared at me silently with dark, unflinching eyes. Surprised, I commanded him to leave in the name of Jesus. Then, just as he materialized, he disappeared like a fading vapor.

I warred the rest of that evening, praying and worshiping God. I prayed throughout the night, armed with the Word of God. Later, I had dreams of his remorse of rebelling against God. In the dream, he was getting sucked into the floor and into the pit of Hell with his hands grasping the floorboards. I spoke to him in the dream, telling him it wasn't too late to turn to God. I saw a flicker of hope cross his countenance like a glimmering sunrise and then eclipse into black. His hatred for God led him through the floor, where voices in agony called him.

Do not wait to repent and give your heart to God. Through Jesus, we have the hope of life and rebirth—the alternative is death, agony, and despair.

38

PORTALS OF HEAVEN

One afternoon, I walked with a friend through the Kidron Valley near Absolom's Tomb. It is the valley where David fled his son Absalom and Jesus crossed on the night of His agony. The valley separates the Mount of Olives from Mount Moriah, where the Temple Mount resides. There are three cemeteries in that region: a Muslim cemetery, a Christian cemetery, and a Jewish cemetery. Scriptures tell all three faiths of a coming man who will come across that valley and split the Mount of Olives to enter Jerusalem through the Mercy Gate. Christians and Jews believe it to be the Messiah, while Muslims believe that man is a formidable enemy.

As we walked the dusty road, I stepped off the path out of curiosity. Two hands started squeezing my neck, trying to suffocate me. They were not human but demonic hands. Christina did not perceive it—I hastened for her to pray in the Spirit. So she worshiped God, and the hands finally loosed from around me. I gulped air, and we both praised God. Realizing the battle we stumbled into, we warred in the Spirit through the high praise of God, declaring God's strength, power, and might, and declaring the power in the blood of Jesus. We rattled the gates of the cemetery and declared God's victory over the powers of Hell. Then, God opened my eyes to see what was happening.

Directly above our heads, I saw enormous angels battling demons. These were not like those I'd seen before; they were huge—hundreds of feet. Swords flashed above me, and the sound of metal clanging deafened me. The angels wielded enormous goldish bronze swords, blowing down the evil forces. The more we worshiped God, the quicker the angels saw victory. Worshipping God seemed to feed the angels a heavenly manna that strengthened them in battle and facilitated their victory for Heaven.

Worship fuels God's Kingdom to be victorious on Earth for God's will to be accomplished. God is enthroned upon our worship—He makes Himself known, inhabiting the praises of His people. Through a lifestyle of perpetual worship and thanksgiving, we become faith-filled adorers of God. No weapon can defeat us when we are enveloped in the Presence of God. Remember, our battle is not against flesh and blood.

Neither are our weapons.

There are portals where Heaven touches Earth, where the Spirit realm is more active and engaged. You can feel it, and you can also help perpetuate it.

Years later, I rented an Airbnb in Spain, and the caretaker stopped by to drop off a few things because the owners were overseas. When she entered, the caretaker became flustered and confused.

"Something feels very different in here."

"That's the presence of God," I told her.

During the weeks I was there, I worshiped God from when I woke until I went to sleep. I interceded in prayer for that nation God stationed me in. I knew Heaven's hosts were with me in that space. It had become holy ground. When I moved in, I took the New Age books on the owner's bookshelves and bound them in the back of a cupboard, commanding unclean spirits to be bound during my stay. It was my legal habitation for the duration of my rental. By the Word of God, I knew I could claim it as my peaceful and undisturbed habitation.

We can claim this for ourselves when we submit to the Lordship of Adonai, the God of Abraham, Isaac, and Jacob. The atmosphere shifted, and the woman noticed. When she asked what was different, I told her she was experiencing the atmosphere of Heaven, which had not dwelled there before. She fell to her knees in tears and started pouring her heart out to me. For a long while, I prayed with her. Over the following months of my stay, she came by often to saturate her weary spirit in Heaven's calming atmosphere.

She was hungry for the peace of God in her life, which was tangible in the apartment.

39

DESERT PRAYER

During the last weeks in Israel, when I wasn't in the prayer tower, I enjoyed being part of the Jewish community. I treasured these friendships, learning about Judaism and interceding together in prayer. We worshiped God. I was not on a mission to convince them about Jesus—I was there because my God, their God, *our* God, called me. He was showing me His land and His people. I went with eyes open and heart soft, a blank slate for God. I fell in love with the Land and the people, just like my Father in Heaven, many centuries ago. I grew in understanding who God is from the Jewish perspective, enlightening my knowledge as a follower of Jesus. It is like many puzzle pieces; only God can fit them together. My faith grew more substantial, and I became in awe of God.

God told me He wanted me to go down the Negev Desert to release specific scriptures. The Negev is the large desert south of Be'er Sheba, encompassing nearly half of Israel. My assignment was to go to the desert and speak out loud to it; I was to remind the land of its destiny and activate God's words from the Bible.

I didn't have a car, but I figured out how to journey for several hours to fulfill this instruction from God. I took three different buses and transferred to stations along the way. When I got as close as I could by bus to the spot on the map I knew to go, I walked a few miles to find the enormous desert crater called Mitzpeh Ramon.

I found it, and it took my breath away. It was majestic, like the Grand Canyon, its ridges and jagged edges overlooking a deep red canyon. I walked the perimeter with my Bible in hand. Standing on a promenade, I spoke over the enormous canyon and released awakening words.

 The Lord will make Zion's deserts like Eden, her wastelands like the garden of the Lord. Joy and gladness will be found in her, thanksgiving and the sound of singing. (Isaiah 53)

I reminded the land of God's promise in Ezekiel 37 that He will bring His exiled back to the land and gather them in. I also read from the book of Obadiah, which speaks of Jewish exiles from Spain returning to possess the towns of the Negev.

I read verses about springs of water bursting forth under the desert, and the creation's anticipation of the return of her lost children. They will come soon; the atmosphere is palpable.

Seeing the desert landscape and walking to a remote bus stop miles from anywhere was amazing. The moon came out, and the sky filled with starlight. Ibexes and desert animals scurried and howled as night descended. I marveled that it looked so much like the Southwest of the United States, like New Mexico, where so many of Israel's lost children fled from Spain's Inquisition. I thought making one's home in familiar topography and climate would be easy. Cactus and rocks were so similar in color and shape.

The faith journey to Israel removed the lid from the box of

Desert Prayer

everything I thought I knew. Before the trip, I knew no one there and had no idea what lay before me. If I tried to arrange my three months myself, it would never, could never, be as perfectly orchestrated as it was. God opened the doors. God made the introductions. God ordered my steps. For someone trying not to be the perpetual planner, I was learning to relax and let God lead the dance of my life. He could have every dance on my card. I was starting to prefer His leading me.

KING DAVID SANG in Psalm 119:105:

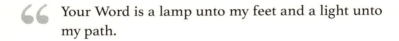
> Your Word is a lamp unto my feet and a light unto my path.

Back then, they didn't have high-beam headlights or flashlights that illuminated football fields. They had little oil lamps that only shined to reveal a few paces at a time. We see how God arranges the details when we focus only on our next two or three steps.

The more we step out upon the waters of faith, the further from the safety of the boat we go. The water is beneath our feet, and we start running over the waves. Because He is leading the way, and it is His delight to take us to new horizons with our beautiful God.

40

THE KINGDOM IS HERE

The most prominent message Jesus delivered was about the Kingdom of God. Jesus hardly talked of anything else. Jesus preached the Kingdom was finally here and was about to turn the world upside down.

What is the Kingdom of God? To be a Kingdom, there must be a King, a people, and a system of governance. Jesus taught many parables about God's Kingdom. He compared it to a merchant seeking fine pearls, a fisherman who threw his net into the sea, and a farmer who sowed seed. He compared it to a woman who put yeast in a lump of dough and a man who found treasure buried in the ground.

The Kingdom of God started in the book of Exodus with a nation called Israel. He created Israel from one man, Abraham, with whom He made a covenant. God's promise to Abraham passed to Isaac and Jacob, whose name God changed to Israel. Jacob's twelve sons became the heads of tribes. One of Jacob's sons, Joseph, became a prominent leader in Egypt after his brothers betrayed him. He became the physical savior of his brothers during the famine, a foreshadowing of the Messiah, who would be the ultimate spiritual savior from death. After a few generations, a different Pharaoh emerged who enslaved the Israelites, and God miraculously delivered them from Egypt and into the Promised Land. God told them they would be a priestly Kingdom and a holy nation to Him, meaning that Himself would be King.

It started in the desert. God has a family plan. Families become tribes. When tribes serve together under one king, you have a nation.

After Israel entered their land, they became jealous of the surrounding nations with visible kings. They complained to Samuel. The book of First Samuel 8:6 says, "The people have not rejected you but have rejected Me from being King over them." God gave them their desire. The Kings were a disaster and led to civil war. After King Solomon, ten tribes split off in the north.

Only David came close to being great; he was the only king the twelve tribes trusted enough to unite under. After him, the nation was divided, overcome by enemies, and taken into captivity. The ten northern tribes disappeared from history. The two in the south (Judah and Benjamin) fell prey to the Babylonians. God's Kingdom didn't exist on Earth for another 70 years. That's why they wept in Babylon. They had been the only nation with God as King, and it was gone.

After seventy years, a remnant, including Nehemiah and Ezra, returned to Israel under Persian, Greek, and Roman rule. What had been God's Kingdom became a vassal state ruled by pagans. God didn't speak.

Hundreds of years went by.

The people who sat in darkness eventually began to see a great light. A man arose in the Galilee. He could speak a word, and the lame would get up and run. Jesus stretched out His hand, and blind men saw. Jesus walked on the surface of the water. He multiplied food.

Word spread like electricity throughout the land. God has

returned to Israel! But this man had much more than miracles. This man came with a message to Earth.

"Repent Israel. Change your ways. The Kingdom of God is here."

Jesus sent His disciples to preach the Good News. There is a King, and His Name is Jesus. Isaiah 9:6 prophesied about this coming King:

> Unto us, a Son is given: and the government shall be upon His shoulder: and His name shall be called Wonderful, Counsellor, Mighty God, Everlasting Father, The Prince of Peace.

This is Jesus, Son of God and Son of Man. When Jesus comes to take the scroll from the right hand of the One seated on the throne, a new song in Heaven is sung, as recorded in Revelation 5:9, saying:

> You are worthy to take the scroll and to open its seals. For You were slain, and by Your blood, You redeemed for God those from every tribe and tongue and people and nation. You have made them a Kingdom and Priesthood for our God, and they shall reign upon the Earth.

This is the good news. Indeed, the people in darkness have seen a great light!

41

MURRE

My favorite bird is the murre. Now, I'm not a birder, and I always thought birders were dorky, peering around through a set of binoculars and usually quite birdlike themselves. But God has a sense of humor and speaks to me through certain birds. I once watched murres at an aquarium dart deep underwater and fly under the sea. Their wings propelled them both in the air and the water below. They were ambidextrous in both realms. I stood fascinated as they pierced from air to sea to air. It got me thinking that I, too, could break out of the box. I wasn't limited to one realm or another; I existed in both. The Bible says we are aliens and sojourners on Earth, that this is not our home (see 1 Peter 2:11). We anticipate and hope for a better place.

Jesus told His followers they were not of this world—just as He was not of this world (see John 17:16). As we look more like Jesus, we become more aware that this is not our home. Like the murre, we fly in both realms, adept and strong. When we stay fixed on Him, we learn to be water walkers like Jesus.

When an heir is young, they are under guardianship until the date set by the father. While we are young in faith, we are subservient to the world's principles. But when the fullness of time comes, we no longer depend on the world's governance because we become co-heirs with Jesus. Galatians 4 explains this. We were infants when we came to faith through Jesus; our destiny through Jesus is that we grow and stretch broader and higher, learning to soar with Him. Our destiny is not to enter Heaven in baby strollers. We are called to join the ranks of brothers and sisters in Hebrews 11 who demonstrated lives of extravagant faith.

God is calling you to step out onto the waters before you. What will you sacrifice to step out of the boat and follow Jesus? Goldfish and coy are the same, but one can fit inside your palm while the other can be the size of a grown man. The difference in their growth is the size of their container. A goldfish in a bowl stays tiny. A goldfish in the lake grows large. If you remain in the shallow end of the wading pool, you can only grow so much. Come deeper; there is a mighty ocean before you. Your feet can't touch the bottom. You may have to leave your friends to follow Jesus on that water, but it will be an exciting adventure as you walk on the water with Jesus. Get out of the limitations of this world. The flow of God's Holy Spirit is not standard in this world's perspective. The dead fish flow with the current of the world. But our call is different, for we are alive in Christ.

SALVATION IS FREE, but the Kingdom will cost you everything.

42

JESUS IN THE PRAYER ROOM

One day, when I was worshiping in the prayer room in Jerusalem, Jesus physically walked into the room. I had sensed His presence many times, trusting He was with me, like when Jesus squeezed my hand as a scared little girl in a basement, and I felt Him silence my fears and lull me to sleep. But on that unforgettable day, I saw Jesus. Like most days in the prayer room, I was setting up my guitar and music stand to enter into worship. I pulled a leather armchair across from me and wrapped it with silky scarves from a prop box in the room to make it like a throne. I placed a scepter and a crown. Then, with simple faith like a child, I invited Jesus to come and sit with me while I prepared to worship.

After several hours of worshiping God, I noticed something was different. I squinted to let light slowly into my closed eyes. A person was sitting in that chair I set up for Jesus. It *was* Jesus. I knew in my spirit without any doubt.

I could barely look into His eyes—they were piercing with too much light to look at directly. My guitar fell limply in my hands. I was awestruck. I realized I had the undivided attention of the King of the Universe sitting across from me. I understood I could ask Him for anything and had His fixed attention. He was sitting in the chair across from me. My mind raced, wondering what I should ask for.

All I could do was gaze at His beautiful face and repeat over and over how much I love Him and how beautiful He is.

I didn't want to ask for things.

I simply wanted to tell Him I loved Him.

No other song mattered, and no instrument mattered.

His smile seemed to extend from one side of Heaven to the other. He contained the entire cosmos, and I felt like I was looking at galaxies. I felt like I was in outer space or that outer space was all around me.

I saw His leather sandals and glowing white robe. He was in blue light, except for His shining face, and His eyes were the deepest oceans of light.

Millions of rose petals swirled around His feet. A blur of multitudes was on either side of Him, embodying praise in body. Though not audible or visible, I could feel it very much there.

He knew me inside and out, and He loved me. I wasn't afraid, unlike the night years earlier when the Lord warned me not to move to New York City; that night, I trembled and wanted to hide from His blinding light. I had so much fear, whether that was the Lord or an angel. Now, I was in awe and mesmerized by Him. Time was suspended.

After a long time, Jesus faded away without moving. I felt undone but filled with supernatural peace. After that, I saw people and things through a different lens.

Jesus appeared again when He asked me to invite Him to dwell fully with me. I said yes, and Jesus glided like an elevator and meshed with my belly like a ball of light as if I were a door to a room. Then, He burst into a thousand particles of light.

Set a chair for the Lord and invite Him in. He is waiting for that kind of radical, childlike faith. When we say yes to God, we are stepping out on the water and trusting Him with eyes of wonder and expectation. We anticipate God's movement and expect miracles to happen.

THAT'S the God we serve.

43

UPON THE WAVES

Welcome to the new normal, where the laws of physics, time, and space have no meaning, where mountains move, time reverses, and dead men walk again. In this new normal, limitations do not apply, and everything Jesus said we could do through Him can be done. He always points us to the Father and represents the Father fully.

With so many assurances from Heaven, we have no reason not to run after God. There is a destiny waiting to be unlocked in you. Use what God has given you to love Him and help others find life in Him. Why would anyone return to life as usual after stepping upon the waves?

It is exhilarating to say yes to God's call. Give everything to Him and take His hand upon the waters. An underground church is rising, and the enemy can't stop it from coming. God's plan is too extravagant and generous for the enemy to anticipate.

The radical heart that loves like Jesus is the sound of one beating drum that becomes a chorus with the multitude.

THE REST of my faith journey in Israel went fast. I returned to New York to sell my house, car, and possessions and continue following God worldwide, wherever He would lead me. I burned my plough and oxen like Elisha, with no Plan B. There was no going back. The few possessions I held onto were stolen from storage the following year. I was sad at first until God told me I no longer had anything in my hands to hold me back. Since then, He has given me many things, including a place to call home for now and a car, but everything is held lightly in open hands, willing for Him to move me and for me to be willing to be moved by Him.

I returned to Israel to live for the next two years and then continued to New Zealand for a second time. This time, I would be pioneering a ministry school to bridge Christians and Jews together in understanding and love. That was a challenging assignment since the nation had just spearheaded a United Nations resolution for a significant anti-Israel sanction. There was an antisemitic atmosphere everywhere, and I seemed to have a spiritual bullseye on me, coming from Israel on Passover with an Israeli flag and gifts for Maori Christian leaders.

On that long flight, my guitar was smashed to pieces, and the message I carried of Christians embracing Israel was not widely accepted. I was supposed to lead worship during the first week with all the students, but the face of the guitar wasn't even attached to the back. Somehow, the strings were still connected, though.

God comforted me and prompted me to try to play it, anyway. I had to bundle the guitar pieces under my arm with a towel. I played to the Lord, holding fragments of wood and string, trying not to cut up my forearm on the splinters. We worshiped in that small chapel for several hours in the midst of a dark spiritual battle. Heavy rain poured down in an otherwise sunny sky the entire time we sang. Buckets of rain—the kind you'd call a deluge. As soon as we finished, the rains stopped.

WHEN WE BRING our broken and humble pieces to God, He is honored. It is like the widow's mite: We give generously from whatever we have, giving Him everything.

44

WHEN HE SPEAKS, THE SEA OBEYS

I had many victories in the years between. However, one area I had not yet considered was the power of God over the weather. I saw Jesus' authority many times over rulers in the Spirit world. When the school was established, God called me to travel around New Zealand to share Israel's role in the body of Christ. God wanted the Church to embrace His Covenant People and His Land. In the planning and prayer for my route and stops, God told me exactly which days to go to which places, from the top of the North Island to the bottom of the South Island. I was told the roads to take and with whom to stay. New friends loaned me their car for the month-long journey. I would drive along narrow, winding roads on wintery mountain ranges with snow-capped peaks. It would be just me and Jesus. When I asked God if I should get snow tires or chains for the mountain passes, He impressed me not to, for He would give me safe passage.

I planned to stay with local believers in a dozen or so cities. I would share with churches and home gatherings nearly every night for a month.

Cook Strait separates the North and South Islands and

connects the Tasman Sea on the northwest with the South Pacific Ocean on the southeast. It is 14 miles wide and considered one of the world's most dangerous and unpredictable waters. Regular ferry services run between Wellington and Picton, and tickets cost hundreds of dollars. God told me to buy a sail for Friday at 9:00 am, giving me a couple of days in Wellington with my host.

I was to start my drive the following day to my first stop: Gisborne, then to Napier, and south to Wellington, where the ferry would take me across on Friday. My friend told me to check the news because a dangerous storm with cyclone winds of 120 kilometers was unexpectedly coming. I was nervous at first, thinking I couldn't delay the trip, having bought the ferry tickets and arranged for a dozen hosts for specific days. The news reported a deadly storm that was coming the next day, starting with mudslides in Gisborne, cyclones the following day in Napier, and continuing in cyclone winds and hail to Wellington the next day, from where it would journey down to the South Island and follow the path God gave me to drive, day by day in precise calculation. Roads would be closed. Winds, rain, and hail would be deadly. People were to stay home with a stocked pantry. I was told I shouldn't go because the highways I was planning could be closed for hundreds of miles, making my trip impossible.

I had planned to leave in the morning. This was an enormous hiccup, and I needed the counsel of the Lord. He told me I was to continue as planned. And He instructed me to *rebuke the storm* and forbid it from disrupting God's assignment. I knew the enemy was trying to impede; it was so obvious, for my exact route to the minute was how the storm was predicted to travel. So I rebuked the storm, praying and asking God to speak clearly. The following morning, I headed out.

My travels to Gisborne and Napier were smooth. I arrived at my host's home in Wellington with twenty minutes to spare, having brought my bag inside before the cyclone winds hit. We sipped tea in her living room, watching the trees outside her picture window bend sideways.

She asked me which sailing time I'd bought for the ferry and warned me that even if they didn't cancel the sail, the waves would be thirty meters high from the turbulence because it takes a few days for the waters to settle. I continued to rebuke the storm as Jesus did. I spoke to the weather and commanded it not to interfere with what God had ordained.

My ferry ticket was two days later for the Friday morning sail. The news reports that all ferries were canceled for Wednesday and then again for Thursday. They have never canceled ferries for decades, and this storm, they canceled two days of sails. The next sail would be Friday at 9:00 a.m. That was the one the Lord told me to purchase. Thousands of people were trying to find Friday morning tickets; God already secured my sail time.

When I said goodbye to my host, she warned me not to eat breakfast because the waves would surely be massive still—in fact, they would be a thirty-meter swell because of the storm that just passed. It would be a four-hour sail on choppy waters. I prayed.

"Lord, I do not want to have rough sailing. Please calm the waters so I can have a serene sail. You told me where to go and which days. *I am asking for Your favor.*"

I parked my car on the lower deck and walked up to the passenger deck to get comfy for a four-hour sail to Picton. The passage was as smooth as glass. I kept looking out the windows to see the 30-meter swells. The water was still and serene. There was no sign a storm had just passed. God's miracles continued. There was to be a snowstorm on the mountain pass. I prayed fervently and crossed. My drive was clear, and every road was dry. I saw enormous piles of snow on the sides of the road and in drifts, but they were not plowed by machines or vehicles. It was just blown off my path to reveal blacktop roads everywhere.

I drove along the eastern shore on the only road toward southern Dunedin. The road hugs the coastline and is at sea level. I enjoyed stopping to see penguins and seals as I drove the breathtaking coastline. God protected me and gave me joy in the journey with Him on my assignment from town to town. One day after my seven-hour drive down the coast, the entire road flooded and closed for a national emergency. Hundreds of kilometers were no longer accessible due to the storm and flooding.

The Lord held back the weather long enough for my safety everywhere I traveled. Immediately after I passed, the weather fell hard. Local believers laughed nervously when I got to Mataura; maybe they didn't want me to leave their town. I released God's word from the southernmost tip at Invercargill, where God instructed me to blow the shofar and worship Him atop a windy bluff. The winds were so strong the birds flapped furiously but did not move forward in the sky. The waters crashed violently on the rocks below. God told me this was the South Gate of the planet and needed to be opened through prayer and worship. There was an abandoned lighthouse with a prophetic sign about a watchman who neither slumbers nor sleeps, which is a quote from Psalms regarding the house of prayer David desired to build for the Lord. Two days after I fulfilled that creative assignment from God, local Kiwi pastors told me they had a similar word from God to do the same. We were partnering together without knowing it. This is how God works, fulfilling His purpose through the body of Christ and connecting His heart for Israel to the nations.

When God wants you to do something, He will make a way. We do not speak out on our authority but on Jesus' authority. It is Jesus who calms the seas and walks on waves. When we walk with Him, when we live through Him, we can do the same.

When He Speaks, the Sea Obeys

The storms did not interfere with God's plan for me. Just like He parted the Red Sea for the Israelites to pass safely, I learned my authority as God's daughter to stand against impositions to God's will for me. It was the first time I had seen such majesty displaced over nature. I never needed snow chains to cross the mountains because the passes were dry, even though the hosts who anticipated my arrival were surprised, for the news reported gusts and hazards on every road I traveled. I never saw any of it. God is more awesome than we understand.

HE DOES what He says He will do.

45

KILLING THE SNAKE

On that mission journey, God directed me to speak out and command the threatening weather to be subdued. I watched in awe as the Lord silenced every storm.

Then the Lord said something to me I wasn't expecting.

"Do you want to see something cool? I'm going to destroy that snake."

He said that, which was pretty wild. He was referring to the snake that tormented me a couple of years earlier, hissing at me to leave, which was a valuable lesson when God taught me the importance of abiding under His wing and only doing what He said. When God allowed me to see that serpent, I was like a girl running to her daddy to hide. The magnitude of the beast was more extensive than anything I had imagined, and all I could do was cling to the pantleg of God. I remember feeling like the little Pippin, the hobbit who ran away from the Nazgul and hid behind Gandalf in *The Lord of the Rings*. The snake was Leviathan—an evil principality. God would destroy it and permit me to watch Him do it. Wow, that's something for which you can't buy a front-row ticket.

I was learning through experience that every battle is the Lord's. I was about to watch the Lord deal with that principality. Like an ant on an elephant, I was about to observe God shake the bridge. So there I was, in that small town on the South Island where it all happened a few years earlier. God showed me His power over a formidable foe. I saw the Lord chop the head off that enormous snake in the sky. I wasn't expecting that. I saw its slimy, huge body flail and writhe. I saw its tail kick and spin and then finally stop. I rejoiced; watching God do that was a great joy. In God's perfect timing, He destroyed His enemy.

As I ministered the next several days locally, the Lord showed me damage caused by the snake's body writhing before hitting the ground. We do not understand some things. But I know God defeated that enemy. There are territorial spirits in the world that God wants to bring down. There are hosts from Heaven that should be reinstated for God's perfect will to be done on Earth as it is in Heaven. We have the privilege to partner and watch our Father as He defeats the enemies of God. We get to storm forward and push the gates of Hell back so Heaven can advance forcibly. We are to plunder Hell and demand restitution, putting our feet on the neck of every serpent in the authority of Jesus.

46

MY GRACE IS SUFFICIENT

After God moved the weather and killed the snake, I was returning to New York on a forty-hour journey halfway around the world. I had long layovers and four connecting flights and was carrying hand luggage, a heavy backpack, and a recently repaired guitar around multiple airports with massive terminals. Every muscle screamed in pain from walking miles in airport terminals without sleep for two days. I was walking through the long corridor in the endless terminal in New York when I got to the end of myself and was about to collapse. I cried out to the Lord to give me supernatural grace while reminding myself that His grace was sufficient and He would strengthen me. I kept telling myself that during the long hours of trudging around airports and carrying all the baggage. I prayed in a moment of desperation.

"Lord, I can't do this. Please, Lord, I need Your help."

As I exhaled the last syllable, an airport worker suddenly appeared behind me. He was pushing an empty wheelchair.

"Would you like me to wheel your bags for you?"

I was astounded at the immediate reply to my prayer. It was the Lord's grace and mercy. I loaded all my bags and guitar into the wheelchair, and he walked with me for the next fifteen minutes, side by side, through the terminal. I wondered why I hadn't thought to ask for His help earlier. He was waiting for me to ask Him, for He already had the answer.

I HAD A DREAM ABOUT AN AIRPLANE. In the dream, I had been trained as a pilot for a rare jet. I got a chance to fly it and did well, but then I didn't get a call to fly for a month, and when I did, I wasn't sure what kind of jet they wanted me to fly. So I refused the assignment, thinking I could mess up and forget which levers to pull or push and in what sequence. I felt that if I made one mistake, the plane would crash. My friends heard my concerns as I vented to the man who called me up to work. Why didn't they call me sooner before I forgot the sequences? Why didn't I practice more during downtime?

Because I refused, the jet was delayed while they looked for another pilot. I sat on the plane as a passenger with my head low. People were angry but didn't know I was the reason for it. I decided to watch the pilot who finally took the job so I could remember how to fly. I took notes on tiny scraps of paper jumbled in my hand. The pilot landed in the water where children were swimming. I somehow got on the nose of the jet, and it turned into a boat. I screamed, *"Get out of the way!"* just in time for the kids to move as we plunged into the water. We were at our gate, underwater. The passengers exited the aircraft in the usual catatonic state. I was stuck between two worlds. The passengers thought I was a passenger. The pilot thought I was a pilot. I really didn't know. God says you are equipped and ready. You can do everything He calls you to do. Someone needs to hear that. He will equip you. Don't second-guess yourself.

What's in your hand? You might think you don't have much to offer God, but you have so much because all you need is a

My Grace is Sufficient

surrendered heart and a measure of faith. Moses was afraid to do what God asked and had all sorts of excuses. Would they listen? How could he lead them? God asked Moses what it was in his hand. It was a staff. God told him to cast it on the ground. It became a serpent, so Moses fled from it. Then God told him to stretch his hand and take it by the tail. It became a staff. God will equip you. He will protect and prepare you. When you walk on water, you create ripples that touch others like stones on the water.

MY FRIEND JIM worked as a teacher's aide with boys with learning disabilities. One day, the boys brought items from home for show and tell. One of his students, Jason, brought a complicated model he had built with his father, which had three hundred small parts attached. The model fell apart, and Jason cried. There was no box or assembly instructions, just a pile of hundreds of broken pieces. He asked Jim for help, but Jim was concerned and unable to.

"I can't fix this; I don't know what the original looked like. But I do know who can fix this—Jesus. Why don't we ask Jesus to fix it?"

Jason nodded in agreement. Jim picked up the pieces into his hands and prayed. With his eyes closed, he felt the pieces moving. Opening his eyes, the model was assembled in his hands. Years later, Jim visited a church in another town to see that Jason was a grown man and a strong follower of Jesus.

FRIENDS IN FIJI told me they were not expecting company when a bread truck broke down in front of their house with hundreds of loaves of bread that would spoil. The man asked if they wanted them. They took the loaves with thanks and asked the

Lord what to do. They wondered if He would send people who needed food to them. Later that day, a large crowd came to their door asking for sanctuary. They had more than enough food.

We need each other and can be the functioning body of Christ when we are willing to flow as one. Once, I noticed a group of tree saplings planted in a tight row. The wind was strong that day, and they were blowing halfway over. They looked like they would snap in the wind but buffered against each other. A little further away was one sapling planted by itself. I watched as it snapped in half, defeated under the violent wind. This is how we should be with one another and be in Him. We are protected from storms when we remain tightly bound.

47

THE NATIONS ARE CALLING

Jesus called His followers to go to all nations, starting in Jerusalem and going to the world's furthest locations. This is the great commandment—to go and spread the Good News that the Kingdom of God is here and that Jesus made the way for us to enter in to all of God's promises—no exclusions and no exceptions, as long as we enter under the blood of Jesus and are willing to let Him rearrange the parts of us that need rearranging. He's in the process of sanctifying all of us so that the radiant bride of Christ can come forth.

Since selling my home and belongings to run after Jesus, He has taken me worldwide to share the Good News. For over a decade, I've lived out of a suitcase to go wherever He leads. He gave me a vision of playing guitar in front of the Vatican with eight or ten people. I saw the whole scene in the vision, and it played like a movie in front of my mind. I played guitar and worshiped God with the group. We were worshiping God and creating an atmosphere for His Presence to rest. The Lord inhabits the praises of His people.

As we did, people watched and came over to us to join in

and for prayer. I got the invitation to go to the Vatican several years after this vision. I was living in Jerusalem at the time. I told God I didn't want to carry my guitar to Rome due to logistical challenges, and if this vision was fulfilled, I knew He would provide the means. I flew to Rome and met a team. There were about eight of us. We had several prophetic assignments from the Lord, including reversing curses. One of those days, we went to the Vatican to pray out front. As we arrived, a stranger drove up as close as they could and ran out of the car toward us. She had a guitar in her hands and thrust it into mine.

"Here. Take this. You are supposed to play this."

I took it. I was in such unbelief and awe. I led the group in worship, precisely like the vision years earlier. I sang a few worship songs in Hebrew; when I did, it was like an earthquake rumbled. The spiritual atmosphere was seismically disrupted. We all felt it and trembled. It was as if we were putting a stake in the ground that reached from the core of the earth to the top of the heavens, declaring the power of the Living God. It's hard to explain, but that's how things are when God moves. On the same trip, we had an assignment to put salt in the river Tiber at its original fount, deep within the San Marino mountains. At the river's source, an ominous bronze plaque declared a curse upon the river, the city of Rome, and, subsequently, the entire world. In the Bible, Elijah poured salt into the waters to heal it.

When I returned to Jerusalem and shared this God assignment with a Rabbi, he wished he could partner with the assignment, saying he had salt from the Dead Sea. He would have given for that. It hit me at that moment—the power of Jews and Gentiles coming together in prayer. Christians and Jews worship the same God. The enemy fears what might happen if we unite our faith in God and stand in unity and love with one another. I would have loved to involve the Rabbi in our work,

The Nations are Calling

and in later projects, we have labored together to see God move. Like the vision of ascending the mountain of God, we ascend together and need each other.

I worked for God for years throughout Spain to bring redemption through the blood of Jesus to overtake the spilled Jewish blood from the Spanish Inquisition. God wanted to bring to light the truth of the dark secret of Spain's wicked past; He wants to bless and not curse, and the verdict of reversal was permitted before God's throne when Spain repented globally for the Inquisition in 2015 and invited the Jewry to return. Although the announcement may or may not be repentant, it was sufficient to bring before Heaven's court to bring a turn-around verdict for God to God establish His Kingdom. Spiritual turnaround is coming to every country and continent. God is awakening the nations to decide which side of the fence they will be on. We have much work to do as a body of believers. We must pray. We must engage with God's heart for the nations. We need to rise up in Jesus' authority and storm the gates of Hell.

I VISITED a place in Portugal called *The Mouth of Hell (La Boca del Infierno)*. I didn't want to go, but God told me to. It faces the Atlantic Ocean and looks like the nose on the profile of a female face looking from the Ancient World out over the New World. Waters gush as if through a whale's blowhole, and every wave launches a hundred feet into the sky. The breath of life, the ruach, comes from the nose. It appeared to be a curse that God wanted to deal with. When I got there, I asked the Lord what He wanted me to do.

God told me,

> "Ask Me what I named this place when I created it at the foundation of the earth."

When He said that, I had a vision as if I could glimpse a little into what that moment might have been like. I pictured the Father and Son laboring with the Breath of God, the Spirit. I could picture Elohim creating the world with vivid color and motion. It reminded me of the origin story of Narnia in *The Magician's Nephew* by C.S. Lewis—how Aslan created the world and how evil first entered it. I asked the Lord what He called it when He made it long ago.

> "The Gates of Heaven.
> I called it the Gates of Heaven."

Then, the Lord instructed me to give the location its proper name from God and to cancel out the incorrect one. I wondered why God needed me to do this. But Heaven is sound-activated—God moves upon sound waves. God could have knocked down the walls of Jericho; He instructed the Israelites to march seven times, blow trumpets, and shout. So I obeyed God, speaking as He told me to creation.

I pronounced blessings over this powerful place of creation—the nostrils, the waves, and the ruach. Within twenty minutes, the matter was done, and God released me. Faith doesn't always make sense to our limited senses, but our spirit is in tune with the Father's.

We learn to flow as One with Him, doing what we see our Father do, just as Jesus did.

∼

WE LIVE in an era when God is redeeming Time, canceling curses, and pouring blessings. The greatest harvest is near, for

The Nations are Calling

God saves the best for last. He is waking creation to respond to His voice.

The rocks and trees will praise the Lord.

And the bride is rousing from slumber to fully engage with the Father's will.

48

THE GROOM IS COMING

How deep your relationship with God is is for you alone to determine. There are no shortcuts to intimacy with God. How much of God do you want in your life? Do you want to be a water walker with Jesus?

Someday in Heaven, we will hear the testimonies that each of us carries. As I have written this book, it has come with trials. I have been healing from stress fractures in both femurs. In the months of healing, I reflect on what God has done for and through me. Somewhat ironically, I've been limited in activity to walking in water to rebuild muscles in my legs. God has a sense of humor in having me write a book with this title. Like a child again, we get to look back and remember learning to walk; every season, we learn to walk deeper with God. We abide with God: resting, nesting, breathing, and receiving.

There is a world of people desperate for hope—people who need to know God loves and cares for them. We accept God's Sovereignty over our lives and become the clay on the sculptor's wheel. The "Fixth me, Father" clay is remade to become an alabaster jar full of fragrant offerings that is broken again and again at the feet of Jesus. This is the aroma of Heaven, a surrender song that plays repeatedly. We trust when the water is so deep that we can't stand. We hang in there when He prunes and replants us. We mend. We abide closely to the root and vine.

Seasons of rest preclude seasons of launching deeper into the unknown. Faith is not knowing what the future holds but knowing who holds it.

Faith must be exercised, not just imagined. Walking on water means getting out of the boat. Get off the comfortable couch. Open your front door like Bilbo Baggins did, and step out. See what adventures await you when you step out in faith.

~

THERE IS the story of ten virgins waiting a long time for the bridegroom. They started to fall asleep. In the middle of the night, there was a shout.

"Look, the bridegroom! Come out to meet him!"

The ten virgins all got up and trimmed their lamps. But five foolish ones did not have enough oil for their lamps. The wise ones advised them to buy some for themselves. While they were going off to buy, the bridegroom came. Those who were ready entered the wedding feast, and the door was shut. The unprepared ones were turned away.

Similarly, Noah worked on the ark for one hundred years, and the people around him laughed at him.

"Look at that dumb guy," they probably said.

But Noah obeyed God's instructions to build the ark and demonstrated faith when his ax swung that first swing and the first tree fell. He prepared as God told him, and in due time the rains came. Then, it was too late for the people to be saved. So it is with the coming of the Son of Man.

When the day comes when the Son of Man appears, and the Mount of Olives splits in two, it will be too late for you to trim your lamp to prepare to meet the bridegroom. It will happen in a moment. Preparation must happen now.

Oil must be stocked up in abundance. That oil is the fragrance of a person who prioritizes time and energy in building a relationship with God. It is kindling one's heart in submission to the Father.

So, stock your oil. The heart must stay lit and engaged, knowing the Bridegroom soon comes.

There is a price that must be paid to maintain oil. Intimacy takes effort. You cannot borrow someone else's. Intimacy is not transferable. Everyone must keep their lamps trimmed and their oil supply filled. Everyone is responsible for staying awake, not knowing the hour, for we know the hour draws near.

My friend Valeria had a vision of Jesus dressed handsomely as a groom for His wedding. He was sitting with His head in His hands and sobbing uncontrollably. She asked why He was crying.

"My bride does not want Me. My bride does not want Me."

We are the bride of Christ, the body of believers from around the globe. Do we want Jesus? Jesus gave His life so His blood could redeem us, so we could have a relationship with Father God. That which the first Adam lost in the garden was regained by the second Adam—Jesus of Nazareth. It is time to live like we love and adore our betrothed. Jesus is coming for a radiant bride. She must prepare. She will not be a child lacking wisdom and maturity; she will be mature, beautiful, and glowing. She will be victorious.

Could you imagine a man giving his beloved a blade of grass to show his love? No, he would present to her an overflowing bouquet—the more flowers and fragrance, the better.

The beloved of Christ should not offer a puny twig of love to Jesus. That would be pathetic. But she should repeatedly break her alabaster jar of oil as a sign of devotion. It will be perpetually refilled in the secret place of worship.

The bride of Christ will open the door when her beloved knocks. She will run with Him whenever and wherever He calls her. She will not be so comfortable in her tidy room to be unwilling to sully her feet in the dusty harvest fields.

BEING a water walker requires tremendous faith and eyes fixed on Jesus. Will you put your hand in His? Will you let Him lead you? Your testimonies will move mountains, helping others on their journeys to go deeper, too. We are all connected. We are all books being written.

JESUS IS the Desire of All Nations, to whom we, the Ekklesia—the Church—are betrothed.

JESUS IS A LOVER AND A FRIEND.
    He is a miracle worker.
    He is a life sustainer.
    He is an abundant giver.
    He is beautiful.
    He is glorious.

HE *IS* THE EVERLASTING FATHER.
    He *is* the Prince of Peace.
    The increase of His government will never cease.

JESUS IS the Alpha and Omega.
    He is the Beginning and the End.

He is the Son of God and the Son of David.
He is the Lamb of God.
He is the Morning Star.
He is Lord, Savior, King, and Messiah.
He is a Water Walker.

And He invites you to step out of your boat and take His hand. One step at a time. That's all it takes to walk in faith—one baby step at a time. You will soon be running and perhaps even flying.

Adventures await you. What ocean is He calling you to step out onto? Will you reach out your hand and take that step? What are you waiting for?

The Kingdom has arrived.

And the King is with us.

AFTERWORD

This book is meant to encourage you to step out upon the waters with Jesus and take Him at His word. Try Him and see He is trustworthy and faithful. My life following Jesus has never been boring. There have been seasons of lack and plenty, quiet and warring in the Spirit, sickness and health. When I am weak, He reminds me that He is strong. When I think of how I could have orchestrated my life according to my plans, it seems so deflated compared to God's plans. I have lived with strangers worldwide who have become lifelong friends. I've had God appointments in the most unusual places. I'm continually astounded at how God connects the body of believers everywhere.

God has blessed me by inviting me to partner with His dreams and taking me places I never dreamed I would go.

Each of us has a personal invitation from God to draw and receive from His refreshing living waters. The reward of eternity is not just a distant promise, but a present reality. We can experience the joy of walking upon every wave now and witness Heaven coming down in our midst.

The Kingdom of God has a different currency. We are not

Afterword

held back by material issues, for we have a God who is above it all. Love is the currency of Heaven. It is also the strongest weapon.

I pray that you are blessed and inspired to trust God for more and step out of every boat He calls you from. May we corporately prepare a red carpet welcome so that when the King of Glory comes, he will find faith on Earth.

Made in the USA
Middletown, DE
07 July 2024